FOUNDATIONS OF A

FOUNDATIONS OF AFRICAN THOUGHT

A Worldview Grounded in the African Heritage of
Religion, Philosophy, Science and Art.

by
Chukwunyere Kamalu

KARNAK HOUSE

© 1990 Chukwunyere Kamalu
All Rights Reserved

No section of this book should be reproduced or copied in any form without the express consent in writing of the Publishers.

First published in Britain 1990
by Karnak House
300 Westbourne Park Road
London W11 1EH, UK

British Library Cataloguing in Publication Data

Kamalu, Chukwunyere
    Foundations of African thought: a worldview grounded in the African Heritage of religion, philosophy, science and art.
    1. African philosophy
    I. Title
    199.6

ISBN 0-907015-61-1
ISBN 0-907015-62-X

Printed in Great Britain by Martins the Printers Ltd.
Berwick upon Tweed.

Marketed & Distributed in the USA by
Red Sea Press
D-11 Princess Road
Lawrenceville, N.J. 08648

Tel: 609.844.9583/Fax: 609.844.0196

Lovingly dedicated to my late father,
Paulinus Obodo Kamalu
and late brother,
Andrew Ihenacho Kamalu.

For Andrew

There was a man
A flame that died young
Shone bright
His warmth touched us all
His life lighted our path

CONTENTS

Acknowledgements	ix
Author's Preface	xi

INTRODUCTION

Origins	1
The Modern	3
The Ancient and Traditional Heritage	3
- Sources	3
- Cosmology	6
- Ethics and Moralality	7
- Ideas of God	9
- The Idea of the Human Being	10
- The Idea of Nature	14
Islam and Christianity	15
Towards an Afrocentric Worldview	21
Foundations of African Thought: A Synopsis	24
Task Addressed by *Foundations of African Thought*	27

PART ONE: BEING AND BECOMING

INTRODUCTION

Principle of Opposites in Ancient and Traditional Africa	31
The Ideas (Aru)	37
- From the Egyptian 'Aru' to the Platonic 'Forms' to the Kantian 'Ideas'	37
Concepts of God	39
- The Ideas as Embodying Concepts of God or Godliness	39
- African Monotheism, Polytheism and Pantheism	40
- God as Uncreated Creator (Unmoved Mover)	45
1. Discerning Opposites	47
2. The Ideas	54
Nature of the Ideas	54
The Theoretical Ideas	56
- The Idea of Infinite Number	57
- The Ideas of Absolute Empirical Truth, Absolute Natural Law and Unfailing Causation	62
- The Ideas of the Continuity of Space and Time	65
- The Idea of Permanent Substance	65
- The Idea of Permanent Self (The Soul and Immortality)	68

- The Idea of the Personal Supreme Being	71
The Practical Ideas	73
- The Ideas of Absolute Good, Absolute Moral Law and Unfailing Will	73
The Aesthetic Idea	74

3. The Arts and Sciences in Africa

Introduction	75
African Science	77
Egyptian Science	77
- Science or Magic? : The Cultural Relativity of Science	78
- Logical Consistency and Coherence of the African Worldview	84
African Art	88
- African Art as a Means of Documentation	88
- African Art as a Means of Concretising the Invisible Spirit World	90

PART TWO: THE SELF AND THE EXTERNAL WORLD

INTRODUCTION	101

1. The Development of Human Consciousness

The Development of Human Consciousness	103
Development of Intelligence in the Child	103
Fundamental Concepts of the Self	105

2. The Cosmology

The Cosmology	110
Ancient Egyptian, Dogon and Bambara Accounts of the Creation	111
Concepts of Space and Time	115
The Physical–Metaphysical Duality: Matter and Void	119
Appendix	124
Discussion of Theophile Obenga's thesis of the primeval Nun	124

PART THREE: ETHICS AND MORAL EXPERIENCE

1. Good and Evil	129

2. Freedom and Moral Responsibility

Freedom and Moral Responsibility	134
Freewill and Determinism	134
Recognising Man and Woman as Ends in Themselves	135
Collective or Corporate Moral Responsibility	137
Moral Conduct	139

AFTERWORD	147
NOTES	161
BIBLIOGRAPHY	174

ACKNOWLEDGEMENTS

I wish to thank my mother, Gladys Kamalu whose selfless sacrifices have given me the space and stability I needed in order to further my work and my studies. I wish to thank the rest of my immediate family, Ihenacho (Andrew), Ijeoma (Angelina) and Chiaka (Regina) for their faith in my abilities. Many thanks to Pitika Ntuli for lively discussions which have helped me to clarify my ideas and broaden my scope and development as a writer. In this respect let me not forget the Jenako Black Writers Workshop. Thanks also to Amon Saba Saakana for his many useful comments.

PREFACE

One of the problems in writing this book has been the language in which it is written. The gender bias in the English language is a source of annoyance to the author who wishes to use a single word to refer equally to Man and to Woman. Even when one finds an alternative to the term 'man', one still has to choose whether to refer to the human being as 'he' or 'she', or attempt to strike a balance through using 'he or she', which can become cumbersome if this has to be repeated.

As Ifi Amadiume notes in her book *Afrikan Matriarchal Foundations*, most African languages do not have this bias. Often a single genderless word is used to mean humankind and one will note that many Africans, in speaking English, often mix up their he's and she's due to the fact that most African languages have a single genderless word to stand for 'he' or 'she'.

The gender bias and the fact that it occurs in English and other languages of the Northern Hemisphere whilst not occurring in most African and other languages of the Southern Hemisphere[1] makes an appropriate opening to the book. The book has as its main theme the idea that the world is ordered according to a principle or doctrine of the co-existence and interaction of opposites on all levels of understanding from the abstract to the concrete. The European world has divided or polarized these opposites. On the most basic level there is the division between the spiritual and physical aspects of human beings. There are also the divisions between the emotional and rational aspects of human beings, the arts and the sciences, man and woman, and so-called 'civilized' and 'primitive' peoples.

Much space is given to describing this *Concert of Opposites* in African philosophy. It is an idea also found in Asian philosophies, notably the Taoist principles of Yin and Yang. There are many similarities between African and Asian religions which might suggest historical connections. Plainly, much more research in this area is required. Meanwhile, the Concert of Opposites is no less Asian and no less African for being common to both Asian and African cultures.

INTRODUCTION

ORIGINS

In 1959 Dr. Louis S.B. Leakey made discoveries which were to imply the origin of humankind on the African continent. Dr. Leakey discovered the remains of Zinjanthropus Bosei and Homo Habilus in association with a primitive stone culture at Olduvai Gorge, Tanzania, dating back almost two million years.[1] Since then further discoveries have been made in Ethiopia dating back 3-4 million years, among others.

With all the evidence suggesting the origin of the human species on the African continent, we should not be surprised by the occurrence of any evidence in favour of an African origin of civilization. A substantial weight of evidence is provided by the late Dr. Cheikh Anta Diop.[2] Plainly and simply, Diop says Egyptian civilization is the earliest history is able to record, and that this was Black African in origin; which should surprise no one since Egypt is and always has been in Africa. Diop cites Herodotus, the Greek 'Father of History' as eye witness.[3] Recently, Martin Bernal, a European scholar, has come to the conclusion that Ancient Egypt was 'essentially African' and that Egypt was the source of Greek philosophy, mathematics, sciences and arts, ... as well as religion. This he has supported by the appearance of the first of three very well researched volumes entitled *Black Athena*, revealing that before the late 18th century the borrowing of Greek wisdom from Egypt was something universally acknowledged and that after this time colonialism and racism had to be justified through the fabrication of the original genius of the Greeks and the comparative barbarity (or else European identity) of the Egyptians. African people were everywhere being brutalised by the European and this could only be justified by denying the Africans civilization and bringing them down to the level of sub-humans or animals.[4]

In understanding the origins of African philosophy it is

vitally important to take into account the ancient history of the people who developed it. European scholars often tell us that the great weakness of our (African) religion is that it has no written text. The earliest religious script known is African: popularly known as *The Egyptian Book of the Dead* and more fittingly named by its original title *The Book of Coming Forth By Day* (also *Papyrus of Ani*). According to E.A. Wallis Budge, this book was in use among the Egyptians from at least 4,500 B.C.[5] and it evidently inspired both the Holy Bible and the Torah (Torah approx. 800 B.C. and Holy Bible approx. 100 A.D.). We see this particularly in the Old Testament and in St. John's gospel in the New Testament. Substance will be given to these claims further on.

The collection of scripts defined by Budge as the *Book of the Dead* embodies most of the ancient African philosophy we know of. Another important source which will be referred to here is the so-called Berlin Papyrus. Ancient African philosophy is the first of what are seen as the three streams of African philosophical heritage: the ancient, the traditional and the modern. The philosophy of *Foundations of African Thought* is grounded mainly in the ancient and the traditional, although some points are elucidated with reference to modern African thinkers. The subject of modern African philosophy is long overdue to be documented on its own. I say this believing that no such work has escaped my notice. For the sake of clarity we need to make a distinction between ancient African religion and philosophy, and traditional African religion and philosophy. Traditional African religion and philosophy, most thoroughly researched by Mbiti,[6] refers to those beliefs prevalent on the continent today for which no history of its development has been written; whilst the ancient refers to the beliefs of the ancient Africans (Egyptians). Many instances of their identity are given in this work. The reader may find these tedious at times, but in the light of past misunderstandings, propagated by European authors, it is vital to make the point, as I do repeatedly, that the traditional is nothing but the latter day form of the ancient. Parrinder[7] makes an allusion to this as mere theory; but there are so many instances of similarity as to defy coincidence

– they are mother and daughter. Furthermore, because of the unity of African culture, for which Diop gives conclusive evidence,[8] we know it makes sense to speak of African religion and philosophy universally as a single body of knowledge.

THE MODERN

Within the third stream, the modern, there are several discernible lines of thought; some echoing traditional ideas, some emerging as a result of the situation in which we Africans find ourselves in the modern world. According to Abiola Irele, there has been a development in the modern producing a body of thought which responded to colonization and identified itself with history.[9] The condition of African peoples was not to be expounded in a vacuum as Europeans had done in a deliberate attempt to mispresent the fact, but in the context of a long history of human and material exploitation by Europe, from the Slave Trade through colonialism to neo-colonialism. These African thinkers (Nkrumah, Cabral, Toure, Fanon and others) were catalysts of social change. The world witnessed the 'Winds of Change' following the independence of Nkrumah's Ghana in 1957. Not only were changes to take place in Africa with many African countries gaining political independence, but the Black Power movement emerged in the States with the Black Panthers. Malcolm X, Angela Davies and Stokely Carmichael (Kwame Toure) all emerging inside a period of less than a decade.

THE ANCIENT AND THE TRADITIONAL

We cannot deal with the modern stream here; but we might give brief sketches of the ancient and traditional streams. Since the latter two are mother and daughter it is at times easier to speak of them as one; at other times no direct link is seen in certain themes, and they are spoken of separately.

Sources

As already mentioned, the chief sources to which we refer for the ancient stream are the *Book of the Dead* as translated by

E.A. Wallis Budge, and the nameless hieratic papyrus 3024 of the Berlin Museum translated by Bika Reed and retitled by her as *Rebel in the Soul*. Budge divides the history of the *Book of the Dead* into four periods represented by four versions. The earliest of these are the 'pyramid texts', so-called because they are inscribed on the interior walls of the pyramids of kings of the fifth and sixth dynasties at Sakkara. Budge gives the name *Book of the Dead* to '... the general body of texts which' (so he says) 'have reference to the burial of the dead and to the new life in the world beyond the grave which are known to have been in use among the Egyptians from about B.C. 4500 ...'.[10] The Berlin papyrus has been dated 2500–1991 B.C. at the earliest, and like nearly all ancient scriptures the authors are unknown. The first Egyptologist to publish its translation was the German, Adolf Erman. Reed makes the following comment about her fellow Egyptologists in relation to the papyrus: '... While translating the Berlin Papyrus 3024 and reviewing earlier interpretations, I experienced awe at encountering philosophical language ever conceived by man, and at the same time felt sorrow at witnessing its debasement .... It is so strange that so simple and evocative a language as ancient Egyptian should be obscured by the very instrument of its rediscovery, the Egyptologist. ... can somebody who believes that Ancient Egypt was a primitive society, incapable of abstract thought, transmit ... its wisdom? ... It is as if a sleepwalker were placed as judge over the awake'.[11]

From the ancient African scriptures we are able to discern our ancestors' deep insight into nature, and a worldview including man and woman, God, nature and society. In these scriptures one will find the early sources of inspiration for the Holy Bible and the Torah. If we compare Brugsch's version of the Egyptian creation myth with the Bible, we cannot expect a word for word resemblance; however, if we compare the two descriptions concept for concept we see them to be almost identical. Take the first three paragraphs of Genesis from the King James version:

> In the beginning God created the heaven and the earth
> 2. And the earth was without form and void; darkness was upon the face of the deep. And the spirit of God moved upon the face of the waters.
> 3. And God said let there be light: and there was light.

Now Budge describes Brugsch's version (in *Religion und Mythologie*, p.101) of the Egyptian account of creation:

> ... there was in the beginning neither heaven nor earth, and nothing existed except a boundless primeval mass of water which was shrouded in darkness .... The divine primeval spirit which formed an essential part of the primeval matter felt within itself the desire to begin the work of creation, and its word woke to life the world ....[12]

Comparing the description concept for concept we see, firstly, that in each case neither heaven nor earth exists in the beginning and there was nothing but water shrouded in darkness. Secondly that within or upon the face of this water there was a divine primeval spirit. Lastly, we saw the importance of the word in bringing everything into being. In the Bible the command was 'Let there be light'. Having said this we must remember that the Egyptian version given is Brugsch's translation and interpretation which are naturally open to challenge.

Additionally, many of the ethical rules and principles we find in the Old Testament can also be seen to have originated from the Egyptian scriptures. The Ten Commandments, for instance, would seem to be no more than later summaries of the earlier 'Forty-two Negative Confessions' (as Budge calls them) or 'Declarations of Innocence' which can be found in the *Book of the Dead*. For further support of this the reader is referred to the *Husia*, a compilation of Egyptian sacred texts by Dr. Maulana Karenga as well as James Breasted's *The Dawn of Conscience*.[13]

Furthermore, there exists another body of religious texts acquired by the Greeks and authored by the Egyptian sage Hermes Trismegistus. One of these, the *Corpus Hermeticum*, says that in the beginning was God (pictured as a boundless expanse of light). Then formless matter (pictured as a cloud of darkness) came into being. The formless matter first assumed form by changing into a watery substance. Out of the darkness came a kind of fire and from this issues the holy Word. The Word is the son of God.[14] This sounds remarkably similar to the beginning of St. John's gospel in which the Son of God is both the Word and the light that shines in the darkness.

The Cosmology

Though there is really only one basic cosmology in ancient African religion, it occurs in many varied mythical forms. As we shall see in the main text this myth is symbolic and not meant to be taken always literally. An essential feature is that the myths are not just accounts of the creation of the world at one point in time. They also signify the ongoing and unending process of creation taking place at this very moment, and also that which is yet to take place. They embody and symbolise all the aspects of divine creativity, not only through nature but also through humans. Everything is in a continual state of change; matter is ceaselessly realising its unlimited potential for change and it is in this sense ceaselessly creating and recreating itself. In the *Book of the Dead* it says:

> He createth but was never created; He is the maker of his own form, and fashioner of his own body – God himself is existence. He endureth without increase or diminution. He multiplieth himself millions of times, and He is manifold in forms and in members – God hath made the universe, and He hath created all that therein is; He is the creator of what is in the world, and of what was, of what is and of what shall be.[15]

'God himself is existence', it says. One cannot help seeing in this the wisdom which was later to recur, through the doctrine of St. Thomas Aquinas, in the west, that identified God's essence with existence. It is on studying the philosophy of Egypt that one encounters further evidence of the fact that much of the work of the so-called great western philosophers was not original and that such beliefs had been held within the religious systems of other civilizations for thousands of years before.

Ethics and Morality

The ethics and morality of the Egyptian scriptures, just as in the case of traditional beliefs, centers on the duality between good and evil; and in fact the foundation of the whole of African philosophy, ancient and traditional, can be conceived in terms of dualities of opposites. We shall go into this thoroughly in the main text. In ancient African ethics (and in science too) there was a single principle which embodied justice, truth and righteousness; and this was called *Maat*. It is the principle of divine order, both in the ancient and the traditional (although traditional African philosophy and religion have no universal word for this concept the idea still exists).[16] This order is both in the laws of nature and in morality among people. Thus the organization of society and the cosmos are founded on the same principle. The human being is seen to be a replica of his or her external universe and it is perfectly sensible to make the analogy between the harmonious governance of society according to ethical principles and the harmonious motion of the cosmos according to physical laws. The duality of good and evil are seen in terms of this desired harmony. Evil is, in the ancient scriptures, known as *Isfet*, meaning chaos; a deviation from the natural course of nature. Thus, as good is the opposite of evil, *Maat* is the opposite of *Isfet*. Needless to say, the notion of evil as chaos is also to be found in the traditional.[17] *Maat* was also a principle of reciprocity in its signification of justice. In other words the moral agent always gets what he or she deserves; every deed, good and bad, returns to the doer. In general, as Mbiti notes, Africans do not believe in reward or punishment in a hereafter. Rewards and punishments are received here on earth.[18]

In the traditional African view moral responsibility is corporate. A wrong done by the individual will have adverse effects on his or her community and the community shares responsibility for the wrong committed by its members.[19] In this regard, if one considers the community of people of African descent in relation to the principle of *Maat* and our current condition of subjugation, one is reminded of the religious creed so effectively used to indoctrinate Africans into seeing their subjugation through racism as a punishment for their past. The case in point is the biblical myth of Ham, for whose 'wrong' all black people, by some accounts, have allegedly been cursed (Genesis 9:18 to 9:27). This belief has led some African christians to heap guilt upon themselves instead of their oppressors. African people have not always been subjugated since the time of Ham, and therefore this myth is not borne out by history. On the contrary, less than 1000 years B.C., the Ethiopian empire spanned across Arabia and Asia Minor and reached as far as the River Ganges in India (supposedly named after the Ethiopian General Ganges).* The Dravidians of modern India are the descendants of these Ethiopians.[20] In addition to this, Bernal cites several authors of ancient times, chief among them being Diodoros, who refer to the Egypto-Phonecian colonizations of ancient Greece.[21] On the surface this appears to point to the African community's subjection in history to the principle of *Maat* although the parallels are not precise. However, it has nothing to do, as the myth of Ham is interpreted by some to suggest, with a racial curse. It implies instead an inevitable cycle of nature to which all beings, without exception, are subject. *Maat*, the moral order, does not discriminate. Those whose rule is sustained by the sword are eventually overthrown by the sword – this is *Maat*.

The opportunity is taken here to mention a similar belief in the nature of history held by Garvey; for Garvey's ideas reveal a moral necessity behind the emancipation of the African race. Professor Tony Martin in his book *Race First*, describes this belief of Garvey's as a 'cyclical theory of history'; since Garvey says, in reference to the resurgence of the African race: 'In the cycle of things he lost his position, but the same cycle will take him back to where he was once'.[22] Martin goes on to note Garvey's humanity in his use of history. Garvey did not

* There is no source to authenticate this assertion. (Ed.)

believe in glorifying the African past, for history was only to be used to instil a lost African pride and provide us with an example of what African people are capable of achieving. He took the view that great civilizations of the past were destroyed by excessive materialism and submergence of human values. The black man (the term Garvey uses to describe African men and women collectively), in Garvey's eyes, had the double experience in history of being first the top dog then the underdog. In modern times the white man is destroying the world through materialism and his delusions of racial superiority. Garvey saw the redemption of an African race wisened by this double experience as a path to the aversion of an armageddon: '... the recovery of the race in its sublimest thought will give it an urge, direct it toward an end that will bestow great blessings upon mankind'.[23]

Ideas of God

African religion, both ancient and traditional, is fundamentally monotheistic; yet it incorporates many symbols of the one God. Africans believe and always have believed in one and only one God whose many aspects are seen in the many aspects of nature as lesser gods of nature. Ancient and traditional religions similarly have gods of the sky, the earth, the sun and the rain among others.

African religion considers the human being to be the centre of the universe. This makes it ascribe human attributes to God. Not that woman and men see God as human, but that God is beyond human experience and the conception of God as human is merely an aid to the limited human understanding. Bodily parts and activities are attributed to God. Some say God has eyes which, in traditional religion, are thought to be the sun, moon or firmament. And some picture God as having a long beard. Most prevalent of all is the idea of God as the potter who fashioned man out of clay. Similarly, in Ancient Africa God's eye was the 'eye of Ra': in hieroglyphics He is symbolised as having a beard: and the God Khnum or Khnemu is the potter who fashioned humans out of clay in the creation. Despite all these attributes God was conceived as immaterial and invisible.

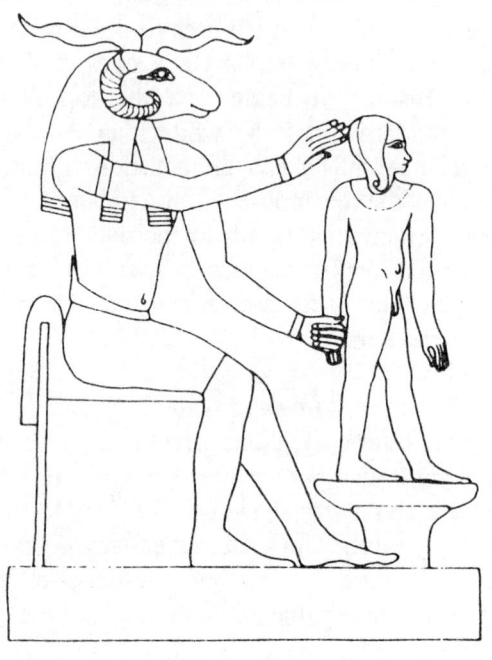

Fig. 1 The Ram-God Khnum.
In Ancient Egyptian creation mythology Khnum was the potter who moulded the first human out of clay. Similarly, in the creation mythology of traditional Africa, God is portrayed as the potter who fashioned humans from clay.

The Idea of the Human Being

The ancient Africans clearly had a philosophy of human striving for perfection through self knowledge. The Berlin Papyrus seems to be all about this. It might appear that traditional African religion has no counterpart of this; but such profound knowledge is often masked by esoteric symbolism. A similar situation does arise in traditional as in ancient Africa, where such knowledge is confined to members of the community initiated into the priesthood. It was understood that such knowledge in the wrong hands could be used to the detriment rather than the benefit of the community; thus the exclusion of all but a few to certain kinds of knowledge was based and still is based on moral considerations. The initiate had to be proven a person of morally conscientious and wise character. No doubt, such a system is not bound to be incorruptible, despite good intentions. However, it may be contrasted with the western educational system where access to specialist knowledge is based upon intellectual, economic and political considerations but never moral ones. Western research follows no moral guidelines; rather, it is controlled by business interests. As a result, the question is never asked as to what consequences new scientific creations will have for the environment and future generations. Generally, the foremost concern is how much money will be made.

The Egyptian education system or 'mysteries', as it was called, involved several stages before one could be admitted to the learning of esoteric philosophy. Greek philosophers who were taught by Egyptian priests, such as Pythagoras and Democritus, first of all had to be initiated and were required to become circumcised.[24] The Dogon of Mali and the Bambara of Guinea similarly have systems whereby only initiates are admitted to esoteric knowledge. Marcel Griaule, the French researcher, had to spend 15 years between 1931 and 1946 living and learning among the Dogon before he was admitted to the higher levels of Dogon knowledge. Before this he was given only the simple knowledge that the Dogon give to unknown inquirers.[25] In traditional and ancient Africa, this esoteric knowledge is not only found in writings (as in ancient scripts), it is found in art and in architecture. In the ancient art, architecture and writings there lie hidden a wealth of knowledge about ourselves and the world. As Schwaller de Lubicz notes in his work *Symbol and the Symbolic*[26] we are unable to understand the language because we would need to adopt a totally different

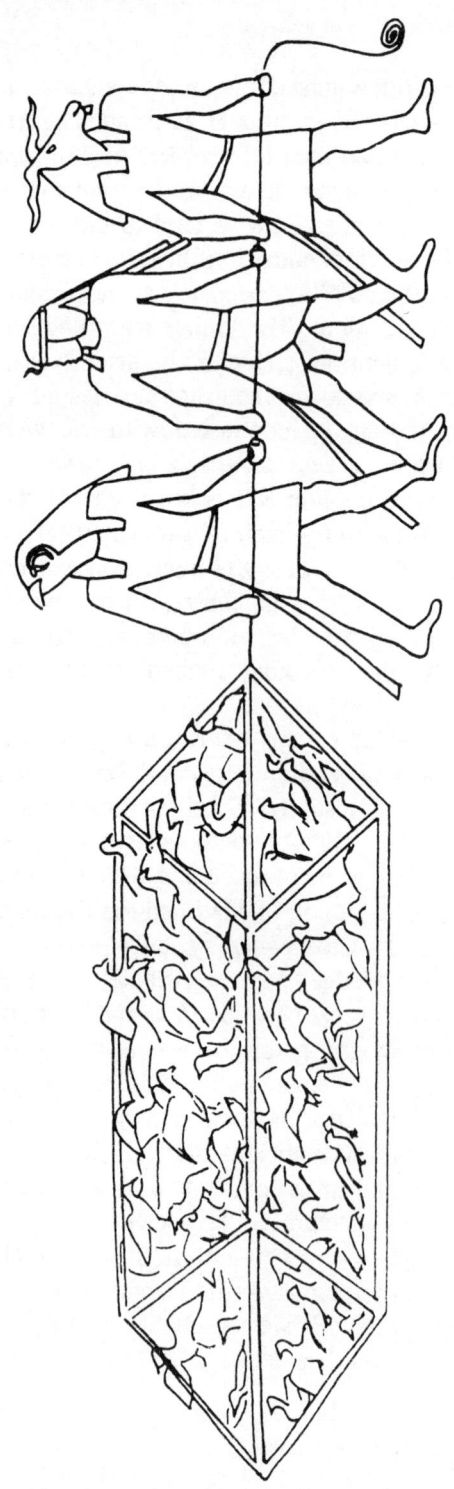

Fig. 2 Birds Trapped in a Fishing Net.
This mystical symbol of ancient Egypt signified the soul, Ba (Represented by the Bennu bird) as being trapped within the finite human body. Spiritual liberation amounted to the liberation of soul from the finite body.

way of thinking in order to do so. Our mode of thought, he argues, appears to be conditioned by the analytic, mechanistic mentality of modern western science. In a sense, modern man/woman has been mentally straight-jacketed by rational thinking. Opposed to this mode of thought is what Schwaller de Lubicz calls the vitalist mentality of ancient Egyptian science. This involved the use of intuition (feeling or emotional sensitivity) in addition to reason and lead to a more immediate attainment of the truth through the use of symbols rather than through a logical step by step progression. This symbolism was embodied in the hieroglyphs of ancient Egyptian writings as well as in their art and their architecture, which Schwaller de Lubicz spent fifteen years studying in the Temple of Luxor, North Africa.

In ancient African philosophy, the quest for self knowledge is seen as a struggle to resolve inner conflict within ourselves. This conflict exists between the soul and the intellect. We refer to Bika Reed's translation of and commentary on the Berlin Papyrus.[27] This conflict between soul and intellect takes the form of a dialogue. The stubbornness and rationality of the intellect are symbolised by the ass named, *Iai*, which will not easily let go of pre-conceptions. Like so much ancient symbolism, this is a dialectical symbol, at the same time consistent and contradictory. The ass is plainly stubborn but we might not associate its stupidity with rationality. Yet in a sense, intellect, because it believes itself to be all-powerful, is stupid. It is this stubbornness of intellect to accept its own limits which prevents man from liberating his spirit. The soul which was regarded as a prisoner within the body was often symbolised as a bird trapped in a fishing net. In order to be free the soul or spirit had to overcome the finiteness of the body. This was achieved through a resolution of the conflict with the body, with the soul or spirit and intellect becoming one. The intellect alone could not lead one to the liberation obtained through knowledge of ultimate truth; yet, paradoxically, reason does lead to this truth, for it is through exhausting the use of reason one realises its futility. The exhaustion of the stubborn intellect is represented in the dialogue between a tormented young man who threatens suicide as a hasty path to liberation, and his dissuasive soul. With liberation comes the assimilation into the divine; woman/man becomes one with the universal force or energy or spirit that is God.

In African traditional religion the human being is at the centre of the universe. Thus, in moral terms, the human being is the root of all value. This is in accord with the ethical principle that man and woman are ends in themselves. This, as the German philosopher, Kant, had realised has to be the basis of any moral theory.

Although the African worldview is human-centred it does not excise the human being from the ecological system. Human beings are very much part of the animal kingdom and of nature. It is recognised that human survival depends on the maintenance of an equilibrium or harmony in human beings' relationship with other life-forms.

The Idea of Nature

In African religion God is both within and without the creation. There is an all-pervading energy or life-force in the universe which inheres in everything. This conception of an all-pervading universal energy dispels the idea of African so-called animism as leading to polytheism. Rather, it is closer to pantheism where nature is identified with God.[28]

The animistic idea of matter is important to note since it provides a consistent basis for our cultural viewpoint on modern science. Each object, each unit of matter is conceived as being a system of forces in equilibrium. Internally, there are numerous forces in conflict which cancel each other out and leave no net resultant force. The object may be acted upon externally and caused to move, but internally there is a balance of conflicting forces.[29] Fortunately for us, though not fortuitously, that is the very idea modern science has of matter and energy;[30] thus Africanising our viewpoint on modern scientific reality, presents no problem in terms of the consistency of the African worldview and modern science.

In the African worldview there exists a natural analogy between the behaviour of matter and that of human society. In nature there are many levels of analogy: between the behaviour of atoms and the solar system, between the individual and the society as a whole, between the processes which take place in the human body and those which take place in the cosmos, and so on. Nkrumah in *Consciencism* makes the analogy between matter and human society. Matter is a plenum of opposing forces in tension, apparently stable and inert on the outside whilst a battle of opposing forces takes place within. Nkrumah compared this state to that of colonial and neo-colonial societies which appear stable on the outside; but this is only an unstable equilibrium in which progressive and reactionary forces are balanced. There is progress only when progressive forces overcome reactionary forces; a progress born out of conflict. A revolutionary situation is thus a dynamic situation; it is not a situation of stability or staticity, in the sense that the society must undergo continual change and reform. Once there ceases to be this continual re-evaluation of the society we return to the situation of unstable equilibrium where the balance could be tipped by negative or reactionary forces.

A more appropriate analogy, however, might be seen in nature in the human body's defence against disease. Nkrumah notes that the negative forces in a colonial state are deceptive: 'These negative forces become the political wolf masquerading in sheep's clothing, they join the clamour for independence, and are accepted in good faith by the people'.[31] In other words, negative forces masquerade as positive forces. In the neo-colonial state this disguise is even more deceptive. We can compare this situation to that of the harmful bacteria which resists the penicillin by mutating, copying the cell structure of the anti-bodies produced by use of penicillin.

ISLAM AND CHRISTIANITY

In speaking of Christianity in Africa it is necessary to distinguish between the indigenous Coptic Christianity which came out of ancient African religion and the modern Euro-Christianity imported along with a brutal colonialism. Dr Yosef ben-Jochannan gives abundant evidence in his two books, *Black Man of the Nile and his Family* and *African Origin of the Major*

Western Religions of the African origin of the chief icons of Christianity. The Egyptian goddess Isis and infant child Horus (whose African names are Aset and Heru) are known to be the original virgin mother and child. The white virgin mother Mary and child Jesus are later European versions, as is made apparent by the many older statues and painting of the black Madonna and child which exist in European churches in Italy, Spain, Poland and in the Netherlands.[32] Thus the missionaries were only bringing something new into Africa in the sense that their creed was a European interpretation of Christianity. From before the arrival of Islam in the 7th century Christianity flourished in Egypt, Ethiopia and Sudan. The cathetical school in Alexandria, Egypt was the centre of the Christian world, producing African scholars such as Tertullian, Origen and St. Augustine.[33]

One needs to distinguish also between Christianity as a religion and the use to which it was put. Religion has, in history, always been a primary tool in the colonization or subjugation of a people. Amilcar Cabral discerned that:

> The ideal for foreign domination, whether imperialist or not, would be to choose:
> – either to liquidate practically all the population of the dominated country, thereby eliminating the possibilities for cultural resistance;
> – or to succeed in imposing itself without damage to the culture of the dominated people – that is, to harmonize economic and political domination of these people with their cultural personality.[34]

In other words, the conquest of a people requires that the colonizer either exterminates all of the people, in which case the colonizer would then have no subjects; or indoctrinate the people into accepting subjugation with little or no resistance, since the aims and aspirations of the colonizer would then appear to be in harmony with that of the colonized, and for the benefit of the colonized. Religion has plainly been utilised to achieve subjugation of the colonised by the latter means,

Fig. 3 Ancient Egyptian Goddess, Isis and son Horus – the original Madonna and child.

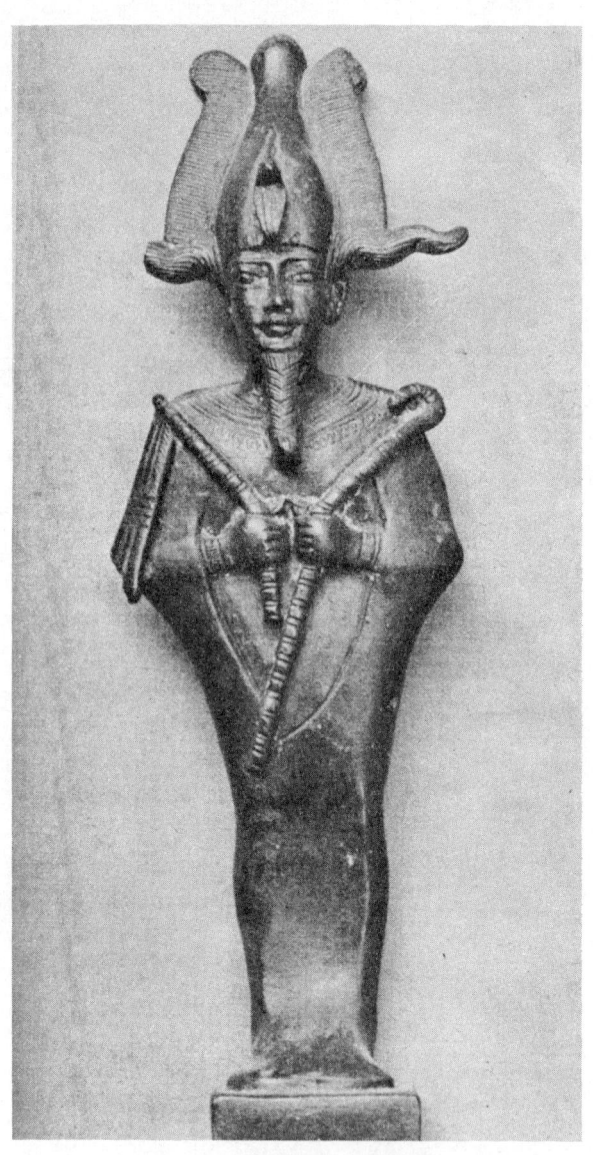

Fig. 4 Osiris.
The first saviour. May be compared with Jesus Christ. He was part divine and part human and the stablisher of righteousness and truth in the world. He was the judge of the dead on judgement day and the giver of eternal life. He was put to death in a cruel manner, but later rose from the dead. (See E.A. Wallis Budge, *Gods of the Egyptians*, pp.149–150)

although colonization in Africa has also involved the element of mass extermination. Cabral believed it was possible (judging from history) to harmonize the economic and political domination of the people with their cultural personality. This is not to say that this harmonization has not been attempted. If we take religion to be the foundation of traditional African culture, we note that the imposition of Christianity along with colonialism, involved not only an attempt to supplant the traditional African religion, but also, through Christianity, the harmonization of religious beliefs and European economic and political systems. In other words, Euro-Christianity in Africa has always existed hand in hand with capitalism. However, this attempt at harmonization has failed in so far as Africans are still strongly attached to their traditional religions. Even where Christianity and Islam are practised we find they are not the same Christianity or Islam that the Europeans or the Arabs practice. These faiths have been Africanised, incorporating elements of traditional worship and even belief. They have been assimilated into the African personality, as opposed to the African personality assimilating a foreign culture.

Islam came to Africa from Arabia after the death of Muhammed in A.D. 632. Its impact has been more widely felt than that of Euro-Christianity possibly because it is less remote from the African traditional way of life. In the 7th century it had covered the whole of North Africa and began to move southwards beyond the Sahara in the 9th century. In a similar way to Christianity, it was a religion used by Arab slave traders and soldiers in an attempt not only to subjugate Africans economically and politically, but to mould the African cultural personality into a form passive rather than resistant to Arab cultural domination. Again, this is not a criticism of the religion but the use to which it was put.

We should also note the fact, however, that Islam, like Christianity, has an ultimately African source. It is a religion strongly influenced by elements of Christianity and Judaism; Euro-Christianity issuing from Judaism, and Judaism issuing from ancient Egyptian religion. Besides this we should also note that according to the African muslim scholar, Al Jahiz, writing in the 10th century, Muhammed, the founder of Islam, was of African descent. Al Jahiz says:

> Abd Al-Muttalib fathered ten lords, black as the night and magnificent

One of these sons is Abu Talib of which Jahiz says:

> ... the family of Abu Talib were the most noble of men; and they were black, with black skin.[35]

Abd Al-Muttalib mentioned in the above quotation is the grandfather of Muhammed; whilst Abu Talib was Muhammed's uncle.[36]

Muhammed's African descent should be understood in the historical context of the region which was originally inhabited by Africans before the 18th century B.C. Says Dr. Cheikh Anta Diop:

> According to Lenormant a Cushite empire originally existed throughout Arabia.[37]

Diop goes on to say:

> This empire was destroyed in the eighteenth century B.C. by an invasion of coarse, white Jectanide tribes, who apparently came to settle among the Blacks .... These facts, on which even Arab authors agree, prove as will shortly become more evident, that the Arab race cannot be conceived as anything but a mixture of Blacks and Whites, a process continuing even today.[38]

Despite the African origins of Christianity and Islam the fact is not changed of their use as tools of colonization by Europeans and Arabs respectively. Today some Africans believing that their faith is under attack defend these abuses of Christianity and Islam by claiming that these are African religions; but what forms of African religion require that traditional African beliefs are denounced as heathen or that one should give up one's African name and take on a Christian or a Muslim one?

TOWARDS AN AFROCENTRIC WORLDVIEW

In my mind, the nineteen eighties have marked the beginning of a renaissance in African thought; a renaissance in which our goal is the liberation of the African mind. It promises to enlighten men and women everywhere through an Afrocentric view of African history which holds great consequences for the way in which future generations will see the history of the world. Whereas before the condition of African peoples was expounded in the context of a past slavery and colonization, we now know that the history of European exploitation of Africa goes back far beyond the slave trade to the time of ancient Greek civilization. And whereas we had previously thought this exploitation to involve only a plunder of human and material resources, we now know that it also involved the assumption of an African cultural and intellectual heritage: that of the ancient Egyptians.

More recently, 20th century western art has to a great extent been influenced by traditional African art, and the western artistic expression known as 'Cubism' was in fact derived, through Picasso, from African sculpture.[39]

Something that is important to note in regard to the above is the racist anthropological theory accepted even by some African authors that either Africans are incapable of abstract thought altogether or that African thought forms are 'more concrete than abstract', thus implicitly denying Africans the possibility of having been philosophers or inventors. The African artistic tradition which is in fact more abstract than concrete in the traditional period in its representation of nature absolutely subverts this idea. On the contrary one finds that it is traditional European art which, before European contact with the African continent, definitely displays the quality of being more concrete than abstract. That is, the work has been more concerned with reproducing or copying nature onto canvass or into stone than using nature as a source of inspiration for abstract ideas.

Remarkably, the foundations of the Afrocentric worldview had been laid even before the first West African country gained independence. In 1955, the late Dr. Cheikh Anta Diop, father of the Afrocentric approach to history, published *Nations Negres et Culture*, the first of three books he was to write for his Ph.D. Diop's views shocked the white academic establishment, averse to anything likely to expose white superiority as a vain myth. Diop had to write a further two books before his evidence was accepted.

The implications of Diop's evidence was quite obviously profound. There lie undiscovered thousands of years of a culturally rich historical past we are largely unaware we possess. Such an immense heritage must surely provide us with a bottomless well of inspiration for future African endeavours of the mind. The redemption of African peoples from the humiliation of the past four-hundred years need not consist in mimicking European civilization. Says Houndtondji: 'Europe is what she is today because she assumed and transformed the cultural heritage of other people, in the first rank of which were a people of our own continent: the ancient Egyptians. Nothing must prevent us from taking the opposite path'.[40]

Houndtondji makes the above statement in a context where he refers to the development of African philosophy by particular reference to the work of Anton Wilhelm Amo, an almost unknown African philosopher who lived in Germany in the 18th century. I mean no disrespect to Amo, but we shall not concern ourselves so much with what Houndtondji has to say about him as with what he has to say about African philosophy in general:

'... in general, what can be meant by the Africaness of a philosophical work?
'Let us say this clearly: our regret does not lie in our failure to detect in Amo's theses that we could claim to be of African origin, concepts and themes that could be said to be characteristic of "African Metaphysics" .... On the contrary, one should readily see how unacceptable, how highly contradictory such an expectation would be. To

require thinkers to be content with reaffirming the beliefs of their people ... is exactly the same as prohibiting them from thinking freely and condemning them in the long term to intellectual asphyxia .... Africans today should be capable of ... freely seizing the whole existing philosophical and scientific heritage, assimilating it and mastering it in order to be able to transcend it ...'.[41]

Houndtondji raises a couple of points which need to be addressed as they appear to be applicable to this very work. Firstly, in regard to his first statement, although we should not expect the African thinker to merely reaffirm the beliefs of his own people he would be in danger of being culturally alienated and speaking in a language foreign to that of his people if these beliefs are not used as his starting point, whether he shares them or not. Houndtondji's approach is a prime example of this. One cannot discuss African philosophy valuably without making concrete references to the themes of that philosophy. Houndtondji fails to do this in his book, *African Philosophy: Myth or Reality*. In the chapters to follow claim is laid to the African origin of various concepts and themes. Though the themes have been interpreted from a personal worldview they remain, for the most part, generally applicable rather than being particularly applicable to any linguistic or ethnic group on the continent. Secondly, it might appear on first sight that Houndtondji contradicts himself in his final sentence; for on the one hand he has spoken of Europe assuming other cultural heritages and urged us to take the opposite path; whilst on the other we are told that Africans must freely seize 'the existing philosophical and scientific heritage, assimilating it and mastering it ...'. However, the appearance of this contradiction is born of the misconception that the philosophical and scientific heritage of the world is basically western, and that in assimilating this knowledge we are assimilating something quite foreign. Human knowledge, although it may be inherited, is not the property of any one race or nation; although Europeans have tried to lay claim to all that is worthy of being called knowledge. It follows that if Europe has appropriated knowledge from other cultures by theft or plagiarization, those other cultures in acquiring European knowledge are merely assimilating a different, sometimes developed form of the knowledge they once had. Houndtondji does not contradict himself for he is urging us to assimilate this knowledge rather than follow the European example of plagiarizing the knowledge of other cultures, whilst denying their contributions to world knowledge. Thus I would not go all the way in agreeing with Houndtondji's definition of African philosophy. The fact that the worldview of an African thinker assimilates a part of the 'western' philosophic and scientific heritage does not deny it its Africanness, provided the thinker uses the African heritage as his or her starting point.

FOUNDATIONS OF AFRICAN THOUGHT: A SYNOPSIS

Foundations of African Thought seeks to interpret the concepts and themes of ancient and traditional African religions with a view to outlining what is a coherent system of thought. It has as its central theme the idea that the world is ordered in accordance with a principle of how opposites co-exist and interact. These opposites have been divided and polarised by European philosophy and the divisions accord with:

(a) the spiritual and emotional turmoil experienced by the vulnerable individual in modern society (the divisions occurring between the spiritual and physical aspects of the human being and between the emotional and rational)[42]
(b) the subordination of women (the division occurring between man and woman)
(c) racism and imperialism (the division being drawn between so-called 'primitive' and 'civilised' peoples).

The 'concert of opposites' is the underlying theme throughout, but around this various other themes are touched. The book is divided into three parts:

(1) **Being and Becoming** – in which the world is seen as being two in one, a duality of the void and matter, the spiritual

and the physical. The spiritual is not manifested in itself but through its opposite, the physical. Mbiti describes this duality as that of the visible and invisible: 'The invisible world is symbolised or manifested by those visible and concrete phenomena and objects of nature. The invisible world presses hard upon the visible world. This is one of the most fundamental religious heritages of African peoples. It is unfortunate that foreign writers through great ignorance have failed to understand this great religious insight of our peoples; and have often ridiculed it or naively presented it as "nature worship" or "animism". Traditional African societies have been neither deaf nor blind to the spiritual dimension of existence, which is so deep, so rich, and so beautiful. The physical and the spiritual are but two dimensions of one and the same universe'.[43]

The duality of the spiritual and material parallels the duality of void and matter described in the text as the noumenal and the phenomenal. These terms are used to emphasize that one is knowable or experiencable; whilst the other is not. All concepts of human knowledge relate either to what is knowable or what is not. Concepts of human knowledge which attempt to describe the unknowable or 'see' the invisible are paradoxical; they reveal the limits of human powers of description and explanation. These concepts are ideal notions known as the Ideas. They seem to be the synthesis of human limitation and the boundless unknown, of the known and the unknowable.

(2) **The Self and the External World**: This part looks at the duality of the human individual and the external universe of which the human being is its microcosmic replica. The development of human consciousness is symbolised by ancient African mythical accounts of the world's creation. In the psychological theory of the development of consciousness in the child, perception of the outside world provides the material with which thoughts/concepts are formed; yet perception also depends on the application of thoughts/concepts possessed by the child. Is conception or perception the first process to take place in the child's development of consciousness or do these somehow happen simultaneously?

In parallel to this, the concept of the self would appear to be fundamental to the coherent human experience or knowledge of the world; yet at the same time experience or knowledge of the world is fundamental to the formation of the concept of the self.

On a more concrete level of speaking the implication of this is moral. It speaks in a symbolic way about the absolute dependence of the individual on his community and environment for his existence and also about the importance of every individual as a strand in the intricate web of life; for the community is, after all, made up of individuals. This points to a philosophy of collectivism, but one which respects the uniqueness and encourages the development of the individual. It implies the natural co-existence of and interrelation between individuality and universality.

(3) **Ethics and Moral Experience**: The human being is the source of all value. It is through his own personal experience that he is able to appreciate the experience of others; it is through his freedom to choose between good and evil that he is human; it is through his action that he may be judged good or evil, and in a manner whereby any action always produces its like, the deed done to others always returns to the doer. It is in the *Idea* of freedom that the physical and spiritual aspects of human beings are seen to co-exist: Whilst each of us individually is totally free on a spiritual (subjective) level, our freedom is only relative and determined by our social and physical environment on a physical (or objective) level. This dual state of affairs is seen as natural, and human freedom is taken to co-exist with natural law. The existence of free will implies that we each, individually, are morally responsible for our actions. However, in Africa, *moral responsibility is collective whereby our actions have consequences for the community – the community consisting of the living, the deceased and the unborn.*

The duality of the individual and the external world is intimately associated with the duality of Freedom and Determinism (relative freedom) of the individual. With this in mind the duality of individuality and universality are revisited in regard to the theme of moral responsibility which is studied from two viewpoints:

(a) *the subjective point of view* of the individual on his own actions, where the individual sees himself as freewilled and therefore solely responsible for his actions and

(b) *the objective point of view* of the individual as an integral part of his community and environment where the individual cannot be considered as solely responsible since he is only a product of his society and environment. This form of collectivism recognises individuality. The individual in African society, being aware of the African notion of collective moral responsibility takes his individual moral responsibility all the more seriously; for his actions will have consequences not only for himself but for his community.

THE TASK ADDRESSED BY *FOUNDATIONS OF AFRICAN THOUGHT*

In this interpretation of the African world system of beliefs it is aimed to show that African beliefs are not a bundle of myths or superstitions without consistency or significance; but that fundamental African beliefs can be seen to constitute a coherent and internally consistent system of thought. Such a system would provide the philosophical foundation for the development of African art, science and ethics. One may ask why such a system is necessary; after all, have we not inherited the western edifice of knowledge? Such a system should not have been necessary had human knowledge been universal and culturally independent. That ethics is relative to culture is quite generally accepted; this is also the case for religion, philosophy and art. However, the case of science is more controversial, due to certain tenets of western science noted by Adams.[44]

1. Science is fundamentally culturally independent and universal.

2. The only reliable and completely objective knowledge is scientific truth.

3. Science is dispassionate, unemotional and anti-religious.

4. Logic is the fundamental tool of science.

5. The scientific method leads systematically and progressively toward the truth.

Says Adams: 'Science – all science – be it the physical sciences, the social sciences or the spiritual (and by the latter I mean music, art, philosophy/religion) is the search for unity or wholeness within or without all human experience. More explicitly, as theoretical psychologist Wade Nobles observes "science is the formal reconstruction or representation of a peoples shared set of systematic and cumulative ideas, beliefs and knowledge (i.e. common sense) stemming from their culture". Thus science cannot always spring from a universal or culturally independent base. It must be consistent with the essentials of its peoples common sense'.[45]

If science in addition to other areas of knowledge then, is not universally or culturally independent, this has very important implications. For, Africans have adopted, through the Western system of education, a science, at least, which has evolved out of a culture which is not our own. The apparent absence of progress in African science as practised by Africans on the continent might be seen as resulting from this cultural alienation of the African academic (apart, of course, from the obvious political and economic obstacles to progress). It is implied that in building a pan-African nation, we must also develop a system of knowledge which in structure and content is consistent with and evolves out of our own culture. This is not to say that Africans must disregard western knowledge. Through our own philosophy we shall be able to appreciate all knowledge (i.e., art, ethics, science, philosophy and religion) from our own cultural perspective so that we may go about creating and innovating in a way consistent with the universal aspects of our culture.

Part I

BEING AND BECOMING

INTRODUCTION

PRINCIPLE OF OPPOSITES IN ANCIENT AND TRADITIONAL AFRICA

The ancient Africans (Egyptians) believed the world to be founded upon contradictions (not necessarily logical ones) and this belief was expressed in the form of the Principle or Doctrine of Opposites. However, to the discredit of Black antiquity and posterity, the Greeks were later to be credited, by their descendants of the European world, with the invention of this principle, wrongly attributed to Heraclitus.

Professor George James shows in his book *Stolen Legacy* that this principle had earlier roots in ancient Egypt in the form of a diagram of 'The Four Qualities and Four Elements' originating from the ancient system of education in Egypt known as the Mysteries System:[1]

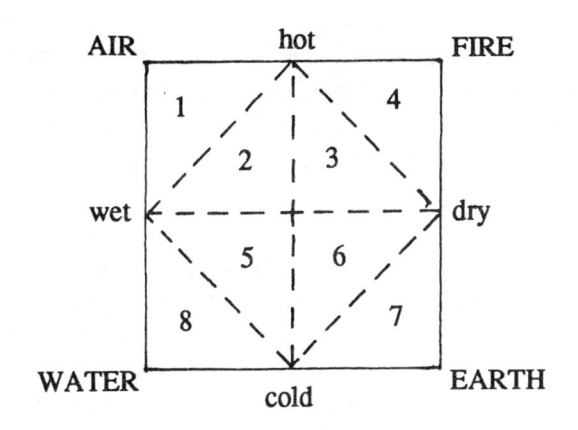

The Four Qualities: Hot, Dry, Wet, Cold.
The Four Elements: Air, Fire, Water, Earth.
(Taken from G.G.M. James' *Stolen Legacy*)

The early Greek philosophers tended to think of the world as constituted by one or more of the four elements, air, fire, water and earth.[2] Bertrand Russell among other European philosophers, speaks of the Greeks' ideas of the Four Elements as if they had arrived at them independently.

In fact when it comes to the overestimation of the Greek genius Russell has only aided in sustaining the myths. In opening the first chapter of his *History of Western Philosophy* he says that '… nothing is so surprising or difficult to account for as the sudden rise of civilization in Greece'. But in the same paragraph he admits that civilization had already existed for thousands of years before in Egypt and Mesopotamia.[3] He goes on to state, that '… they invented mathematics and science and philosophy'. But had he taken note of Herodotus he would have realised that Pythagoras learnt much from his association with the Egyptians. Russell could not have considered the Egyptian thought represented in the *Book of the Dead* to constitute philosophy. Whenever the Egyptians are mentioned there seems to be a determination on Russell's part to divest them of any contribution they have made to civilization so that the myth of Greek genius is sustained. In the second chapter he says 'Thales is said to have travelled in Egypt, and to have thence brought to the Greeks the science of geometry. What the Egyptians knew of geometry was mainly rules of thumb, and there is no reason to believe that Thales arrived at deductive proofs, such as later Greeks discovered'.[4] In other words, Russell is upholding the prevailing idea in European intellectual circles that Egyptian mathematics was not 'real mathematics'; instead it was thought to be merely speculative (i.e., a case of guesswork) as opposed to being deductive. However, the evidence provided by the 'Papyrus of Moscow'[5] refutes this. The papyrus, which is almost 2000 years older than Greek civilization, contains Egyptian hieroglyphic writings of mathematical problems, one of which contains the formula for the volume of a truncated pyramid, something which could not possibly be arrived at by mere guesswork. Another problem on the same papyrus contains the formula for the surface area of a sphere.[6]

In connection with the diagram of the Four Elements and

Four Qualities and the principle of opposites, we note that the same four elements feature in West African religion. In the cosmology of the Dogon of South-East Mali, there was inside the tiny seed, *Kize Uzi* – the original germ of life – an oblong metal plate divided into four sectors, each placed under the direction of one of the four elements, air, fire, water and earth.[7] Furthermore, the diagram of opposites (i.e., the figure featuring the Four Elements and the Four Qualities) is divided into eight sections; eight is a symbolic number for the Dogon – it is the number of original Dogon ancestors, four of whom were male and four of whom were female.[8] We find that in Egyptian cosmology ... 'Under the influence of Thoth, or that form of the divine intelligence which created the world by a word, eight elements, four male and four female, arose out of the primeval Nu (void or primeval water), which possessed the properties of male and female'.[9] These elements or gods were as follows:

Nu and Nut – male and female counterparts of the primeval spirit.[10]

Hehu and Hehut – connected with the word 'Heh' which represents an unlimited number.[11] They might be taken to represent the infinity of the boundless primeval water.

Kekui and Kekuit – male and female powers of the darkness which covered the primeval abyss of water.[12]

Kerkh and Kerkhet – male and female powers of nature in repose.[13]

The -t ending signifies the female form of the element/god.

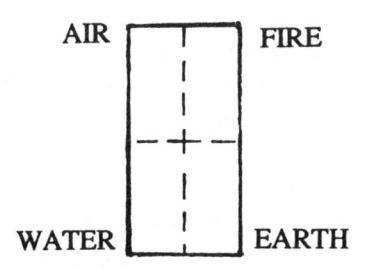

```
AIR  ┌──┬──┐  FIRE
     │  │  │
     ├──┼──┤
     │  │  │
WATER└──┴──┘  EARTH
```

THE OBLONG METAL PLATE INSIDE
THE ORIGINAL SEED OF LIFE, *KIZE UZI*

The oblong metal plate inside the original seed of life, *Kize Uzi*.

Also we can compare the names of the Egyptian gods Nu and Ammon with the Dogon gods Nummo and Amma. Even their significance is the same. In both religions Nu and Nummo are the word-seed or primeval water spirit; whilst Ammon and Amma represent the high God, the almighty.

In this first part we are concerned with the very basis or foundation of experience (thought is included as being a subjective form of experience); for it is only through experience that we know the world. Everything which can be meaningfully said to exist in space and time must possess at least the possibility of being experienced by the senses or as a conception of the imagination. Everything thinkable and sensible will be known here as phenomena or simply, *things*.

The African principle of opposites leads us to a fundamental duality at the foundation of nature. Just as there is a phenomenal aspect of the world (i.e., that aspect which is conceived as being within space and time) which *is* subject to experience, there exists a noumenal aspect which *is not*, but in which we find the ground or basis of the phenomenal world. Likewise, the phenomenal world, by the principle of opposites, is also the basis of the existence of the noumenal. The phenomenal refers to 'thingness', to matter; whereas the noumenal does not. Thus we have at the foundation of nature 'thingness' and 'nothingness'. There is therefore no *thing* which exists as the basis for our world, but there is the concept basis of nothingness, an essence or quality rather than a thing.[14]

The existence of nothingness is made necessary (inevitable) – because of the principle of opposites – by the existence of thingness; for in consideration of any two opposites, it is clear that one cannot exist meaningfully without the other. For example, what would be the meaning of light if there were no such state as darkness, or goodness if there were no evil? The fact that in apprehending objects in experience we have the initial notion (before we have fully seen the object) of something 'being there'[15] inevitably implies the possibility of a state of something '*not* being there'. In the place of an absent phenomenon we can sensibly think of there being empty space, nothingness. This is not in the sense of conceiving nothingness in itself, but through the noticed absence of an object.[16] For example, if I notice the absence of a clock from its usual place on the mantlepiece, I conceive of nothingness through the absence of the clock.

The phenomenal world of experience continually changes, it is never one thing but is always becoming another. For this reason it falls under the class of *becoming*. On the other hand, nothingness, the noumenal world is not subject to experience; but it exists of necessity (it must exist for the existence of things to be conceptually possible) and therefore falls under the title of *being*. Although the term *becoming* sounds consistent in being a reference to everchanging phenomena, it might seem paradoxical for *being* to refer to nothingness, the incorporeal, what most would prefer to describe as *non-being*. However, we should not take substance or corporeality to be the criteria of existence; nothing implies this should be the case. Besides, as we have already noted, we are not referring to nothingness in itself, but in reference to the absence of an object. This concept relating to absence means that *being* may be thought of meaningfully in terms of an existing order in nature where all things are conceived as having 'their place'. This makes obvious sense, as no two things can occupy the same place at the same time.

In order to evoke some insight into the nature of the duality, the reader may be presented with opposing pairs of associated words:

Being	**Becoming**
Nothingness	Matter (thingness)
Formlessness	Form
Infinity	Finiteness
Constancy, continuity	Change, discontinuity
Inertia	Interaction
Stillness	Motion
Everlastingness	Death/birth
Female (male)	Male (female)

Apart from the interaction which ceaselessly takes place amongst phenomena, there is an interaction at a more fundamental level between the noumenal and the phenomenal which is the initiator of the interaction among things. It is not, however, a physical interaction which takes place in time and space: but rather, one which comes about by the mere fact of the co-existence of the duo. In the same way that Good gives meaning to Evil, and Evil to Good, nothingness lends meaning from the material world and returns it. Out of this interaction comes the Life Force which cannot be wholly ascribed to either the noumenal or the phenomenal in isolation. The Life Force is the author of motion and change; but there is motion only in relation to stillness; there is change only in relation to constancy and uniformity.

The opposition of *being* to *becoming* does not involve one being superior to the other but both being mutually complimentary and of equal importance. This idea of a duo at the foundation of nature has survived to this day in various forms on the African continent. One would expect that if the Africans of today inherited their philosophy from ancient Egypt, then this fundamental conception of nature could not fail to be retained. Davidson notes that 'whatever the precise symbolism it is the interacting duality that is always fundamental'.[17]

Various West coast and Nilotic Africans see this as a duality projected by two great spirits. The Bambara of Eastern Guinea see this as Pemba and Faro (Heaven and Earth)[18] whose interaction spells conservation and change.[19] The Dogon have a duality, Amma and Nummo. Nummo emanates from Amma, the High God. Nummo symbolises water and the Divine Word which brought everything into being.[20] The Fon of Dahomey have a duality in Mawu-Lisa;[21] the Shilluk of Sudan, a duality in Juok which is 'from one side spirit (wei), and from the other side spirit, but from front and back he is body (del)'.[22] Each case may be compared with the duality of *being* and *becoming*. For the Diola of Southern Senegal *being* signifies that everything has its order and place in nature; whilst *becoming* signifies the interaction among things.[23] In almost every case the product of *being* and *becoming* is the Life Force, that which gives rise to change and motion (it has a similar role in ancient Egyptian religion as the God and demi-urge, Ra). The Life Force is also the organising power bringing order to the primeval chaos. This Life Force is probably best exemplified by the Fon conception of Da, '... a semi-personal power, ... acting at once as instrument and as conscious assistant in the work of ordering the world. This organizing power, this force of life and motion, is sometimes described as the first created being ...'.[24] Within this concept of Da as a conscious assistant we notice another conception common to Bambara and ancient Egyptian cosmogony. This is the concept of a Divine Intellect which had already thought out, before the inception of the universe, the form which it would take. This is represented in Bambara cosmology by the pair Zo/Yo and in Egyptian cosmology by the god Thoth, the divine intelligence which uttered the Word that brought all into being. This is precisely the same as what the Greeks knew as the Nous. To sum it all up, this interaction of the duality is the fundamental principle of creation which is, in both ancient Egyptian and traditional African thought, a continuous process taking place at this very moment.

THE IDEAS (ARU)

From the Egyptian 'aru' to the Platonic 'Forms' to the Kantian 'Ideas'.

After reflections and discussions of the fundamental duality for which the Principle of Opposites has been the basis, we become concerned with the notions that condition, so it is claimed, the very manner in which we are able to think and to reason. They represent the limits of reason itself. Such are the Ideas, notions of a fundamental nature which are also paradoxical; because man and woman create them unconsciously[25] as a result of the duo of opposites at nature's foundation of which they are intuitively aware. The various Ideas have in common the fact that they might be looked upon as the various conceptions of God or godliness, for each of them is in some sense an absolute of nature. Their paradoxical nature is taken to derive from their being the result of the association of opposite conceptions. The first example that comes to mind is the Idea of a personal Supreme Being. On the one hand this personal Idea of God entails the concept of a person, a human being in essence limited and fallible; but on the other hand it also entails the notion of the infinite and all-powerful, of what we cannot even conceive.[26] We find in this, as in every other instance of the Idea, that the notion of what we have defined as phenomenal (in this case, human being, the state of being limited) and the notion of what we have defined as noumenal (the state of being unlimited) have been associated to produce a paradox. It seems as we shall see in the following pages, that all knowledge is founded upon these types of paradox; for the Ideas are indispensable to us in our attempts to make sense of the world about us. [27]

The Ideas described appear to follow closely in the footsteps of Kant's Transcendental Ideas as presented in his *Critique of Pure Reason*. Like the Kantian Ideas they are ideal standards which have a legitimate function in inducing us to strive towards perfection (whether morally, aesthetically or technically); but they are also unattainable. Unlike the Kantian Ideas they are not solely known by intuition, but have a development which is fostered by experience.

We know that Kant's notions of the Idea grew out of what he had learnt from reading Plato's *Republic*. In Plato's *Republic* the Ideas are referred to as 'forms' in the text. There are numerous references in the Egyptian texts to forms (aru). As in the Platonic meaning, everything possesses a form which is in heaven: 'Thou art crowned with a heavenly form, the Only one provided (with all things)'.[28] Also in the Platonic meaning, form does not seem to refer to mere shape, but to the essence or being of a thing (that is, to what makes that thing what it is):

> 'I know your forms which are not known which come into being with you'.[29]
> '... deliver thou Nebseni, the lord of devotion, from God that secret of form'.[30]
> 'Thou hast received the form of God, thou hast become great therewith before the gods'.[31]

Aristotle's forms (though he is supposed to have ridiculed Plato's Ideas) seem to be in the same vein of thought as the Platonic forms or Ideas. The resemblance of Aristotelian thought to that found in the Egyptian texts is quite striking.

An important concept in Aristotle's theory of forms lies in his distinction between potentiality and actuality; whereas matter without form is a potentiality, matter with form has been actualised. He uses the example of a sculptor who gives form to a mass of stone. The unsculptored stone has potential to become a statue; not until the statue has attained its final form is this potential actualised. This very concept attributed to Aristotle's genius is apparent in ancient Egyptian cosmology. The reader only needs to compare the Aristotelian theories with Egyptian accounts of the creation given in the introduction of E.A. Wallis Budge's *Egyptian Book of the Dead* (p.xcvii–c). There (and in the main text) we find reference to the world as beginning from primeval or unformed matter. At a stage in the creation, Khepera, the god of potential development, brings the inert primeval matter to life. The potentiality is fully realised in almost the manner Aristotle has exemplified by the sculptor, when the god Khnemu, portrayed as a potter,[32] moulds nature and man into their final forms. We find that the notion of potentiality is also conceived in the primeval matter in the sense that it contained within it the embryo of everything which was to come into being. Thus we conclude that the lines of thought behind the Platonic concept of the 'Ideas' and the Aristotelian concept of form had already emerged in the Egyptian *Book of Coming Forth By Day (Book of the Dead)* at least 4,000 years before Aristotle.

CONCEPTS OF GOD

The Ideas as Embodying Concepts of God or Godliness

As we shall soon discover, the Ideas embody various concepts of God or godliness. Many of these can be seen as associated with the ideal conception of a one and only personal God. This concept qualifies as an Idea itself and is more widely used among believers than impersonal concepts. It seems that God as an impersonal concept (e.g., as the void in Buddhism and Hinduism or as Nature or the Universe, etc.) is more unreachable and less understandable. The conception of God as a person seems far easier to grasp and perhaps lends more meaning to any conceived relationship between God and humankind.

To find the roots of these basic concepts we need to look beyond the Greeks and Judaism. In fact these concepts are so basic to man and woman that one wonders if they could have been 'invented' by any race let alone a European one; for is it not more likely they arise by the very nature of human thought?

For the Egyptians there was one, immaterial and unknowable God who was, however, also personalised and whose myriad aspects were symbolised by a company of lesser gods, each of which was limited in the sense of symbolising just one aspect of God's nature or of nature itself. Thus ancient African religion was monotheistic and this among other concepts of God clearly presents itself in the *Book of Coming Forth by Day*. However, it would be to over simplify the religion to say merely that it is monotheistic. African religion is at the same time also *symbolically* polytheistic and pantheistic.

African Monotheism, Polytheism and Pantheism

Certain parts of the *Book of the Dead* might seem to evince the Egyptian religion as plainly polytheistic (i.e., that the Egyptians believed in and worshipped many *Gods*, as opposed to *gods*), but these begotten gods were merely symbols of the one and only God, Amon. Ra, for instance, was the sun which was not worshipped in itself, but as a manifestation of God's power. Like traditional African religion in general, Egyptian religion is almost as Champollion-Figeac describes: 'a pure monotheism, which manifested itself externally by a symbolic polytheism'.[33] The monotheism of Egypt (i.e., the Egyptian belief in and worship of one almighty God) pre-dates the pharaoh Akhenaton (Amenophis iv) who lived about 1400 B.C. We find ample evidence of Egyptian monotheistic belief in the *Book of Coming Forth by Day*, known to be in use among the Egyptians from (according to Budge) 4500 B.C.[34] In western history the Jews are credited with 'inventing' monotheism. But in fact, they were in Egypt when Akhenaton, possibly to promote political centralism through religious centralism, had moved to restore the place of monotheism in Egyptian religion.[35] Most likely Moses (himself an African) was influenced by this reform and then went on to introduce it among the Jews. Whatever the case, the monotheistic idea existed long before the birth of Moses; for one finds statements in ancient Egyptian texts like the following: 'God is one and alone and none other existeth with Him ...';[36] '... thou One, thou only One whose arms are many ... thou One, thou only One who has no second ...';[37] '... thou only One, thou mighty One ...';[38] '... thou art the only One ...'.[39]

Thus African religion, ancient and traditional can almost be described in the words of Champollion-Figeac as 'a pure monotheism which manifested itself externally by a symbolic polytheism'. I say '*almost*' because it is not a pure monotheism in the sense that it also has a pantheistic aspect (pantheism being the belief that God exists in everything and that the world as a whole *is* God, i.e., God *is* nature as opposed to being separated from nature). The monotheism in African religion, however, does not conflict with its pantheistic aspect. They are complementary in the sense that the African concept of God (which is of course prevalent in other religions of the world) is of a Universal Being or Force that is at the same time both immanent (i.e., within all things) and transcendent (i.e., beyond all things as individuals). Immanence in this concept refers to the pantheistic aspect of God which concerns the Universal Being (Force or Energy) that resides in everything about us and within us; whilst transcendence refers to the monotheistic aspect of God which concerns the Universal Being/Force/ Energy that is nature itself in its infinity. The term 'Being' is used interchangeably with that of 'Force' and 'Energy', for in African religion these concepts are one and the same.[40] These ideas will be expounded in the chapter on 'The Arts and the Sciences in Africa'.

Unlike the monotheism/pantheism dichotomy there does exist a conflict between monotheism and polytheism. But, as has already been noted, African polytheism is generally only symbolic. Other authors have varied views. Newell Booth, looking at *God and the Gods in West Africa* sees a tension between monotheistic and polytheistic belief. This is a tension between the ultimate and the concrete;[41] between that which cannot be seen, heard or touched and that which is encountered in our everyday lives. He notes that belief in a supreme being relates to the ultimate; but because this being cannot be encountered concretely there becomes a need for polytheism to counter this inability to concretise the ultimate or know the unknowable. We can distinguish Booth's views clearly from those arrived at above in which all African religion is seen as a monotheism manifested externally by a merely *symbolic* polytheism. In distinction from this Booth concludes that whether Africans are monotheists or polytheists depends largely on which aspects of their beliefs are emphasized. He says Africans '... have not escaped the tension between the ultimate and the concrete'.[42] However, Booth seems to ignore the fact that in relation to the African concept of God as being at the same time immanent and transcendent, the concrete is the expression or manifestation of the ultimate; meaning that the concrete is therefore only seen as symbolic of the ultimate. Perhaps Booth has this in mind; but there is no conflict or tension between a symbol and that which it symbolises. On the contrary, this would be a harmonious and complementary relationship. Booth would appear to be saying that African people sometimes mistake the concrete for the ultimate or the symbol for the real thing, which is not the case.

It could rather be noted that the tension which exists in African religion, as it does in religion generally, exists between the personal and the impersonal concept of the supreme being. The impersonal concept of the supreme being in Africa is that of an all-pervading Universal Force/Energy which is manifest as nature itself. This concept is highly abstract, since nature in all its infinite magnitude is beyond human imagination. However, in order to aid human comprehension the personal concept arises where the supreme being is personified as a human being and as working in ways that are human. Thus this tension arises not because Africans believe that God is a human being, but because the invisible, in order to be made visible and conceivable to the limited human imagination is clothed in the human form. It is very much a case of human beings creating God in their own image.

Imasogie compares the role of the supreme being to the role of a king and his ministers. He says: 'The Supreme Being created the divinities and appointed each of them to take charge of a specific department of nature to be governed in accordance with his order and to receive sacrifices on his behalf. The result is that Nigerians become more familiar with these ministers than with the ultimate source of both man and the divinities. Hence "bureaucratic monotheism" appears the only term that does justice to the Nigerian concept of the Supreme Being and the de facto prominence given to the divinities in the religious expression'.[43]

Imasogie's description is an example of a personalised conception of the supreme being. The role of the supreme being is made to be that of a king with ministers. Mythology in Africa concretises the abstract, and therefore uses a personal as opposed to impersonal concept of God. Imasogie speaks in a mythological form which is not to be taken literally, but rather symbolically. There is clearly only one Supreme Being in African religion, but the many aspects of the Supreme Being are represented by the divinities. Thus in mythological terms they can be logically represented by ministers in a government, given charge of the various departments of nature.

Finally, the subject of African pantheism needs to be revisited. It is more widely known as 'animism' which has in the past been used in a derogative manner to denote beliefs which were mistaken as 'primitive'. In a respected dictionary of philosophy we find the following definition of 'animism' which clearly reveals how racist attitudes have demeaned what is really a highly sophisticated philosophical concept:

> The view that everything in the Universe, including even plants and inanimate objects, has some kind of psychological being more or less tenuously similar to that of human

and non-human animals. Thus it is asserted that a stone is not only an aggregate of moving molecules but has 'awareness' of other bodies in, for example, attracting and repelling them or being affected along with them by gravity. When this theory is held by primitive peoples, it is called animism. Philosophical animists have often been described, more politely, as 'pan-psychists'.[44]

In the same dictionary we find the following definition of 'pan-psychism':
'The theory that holds that the world is rendered more comprehensible on the assumption that every object is invested with a soul or mind. Like the related doctrines of animal soul and world soul, the theory is anti-materialist .... In various forms pan-psychical views are evident in the philosophy of Liebniz and Schopenhauer. The most notable modern proponent of the theory has been A.N. Whitehead'.[45]

African pantheism, although it involves the notion of a world soul or all-pervading vital force, is not anti-materialist. The existence of the spiritual is complementary and not in conflict with the existence of matter. Spirit is pure energy, and matter is its physical form.

Nkrumah distinguishes between the materialism involved in his philosophy of *Consciencism* and the Western materialism which implies the sole existence of matter:

> ... the primary reality of matter must either deny other categories of being, or else claim that they are one and all reducible ... to matter. ... In a materialist philosophy admitting the primary reality of matter, if spirit is accepted as a category of being, non-residual reduction to matter must be claimed.[46]

In other words, Nkrumah's *Consciencism* differs in its materialism from that of Western philosophy, which claims the sole reality of matter, in that other categories of being are ultimately reducible to matter. Thus spirit is an aspect of matter. This brings to light the basic difference between the African and

Western world views. For the African, matter is a living entity endowed with vital force; whereas the Western view is that of matter being inert or dead. Barrett's following description of the African world view serves to support this:

> The African world view is dynamic. The universe is a vast system ... alive because it is energised by a spiritual force emanating from the Supreme Being. This force is allotted hierarchically. Flowing from the Supreme Being, it descends to man and through man to all things lower on the scale of life. Man's very being depends upon maintaining a harmonious relationship between himself, his God, and the nature that surrounds him. As long as the vital force which emanates from God is operative throughout the system and in proper proportion, the universe is considered to be in ritual equilibrium. This dynamic concept of the universe is generally referred to by older writers as 'animism', which is not a bad term if used properly – that is, if used to indicate the organic unity of the world wherein all the parts work together yet are dependent on one life source.[47]

Some may wonder where the pantheistic aspect lies in such a description of the term 'animism'. It is not so apparent here because of Barrett's insistence on separating the Supreme Being from His(Her) Creation. The all-pervading spiritual force, it is contended here, *is* the Supreme Being as opposed to being something which emanates *from* the Supreme Being, and nature in its material mode, that is, everything we see around us is the manifestation of this invisible spiritual force.

God as Uncreated Creator (Unmoved Mover).

From examining ancient Egyptian cosmology it is apparent that western philosophy has falsely attributed the doctrine of the Unmoved Mover to Aristotle: 'I am he who evolved himself under the form of the god Khepera, I, the evolver of evolutions evolved myself ...'[48] And in Brugsch's interpretation of the Egyptian creation account we are told: 'When the inert mass of primeval matter felt the desire of the primeval spirit to begin the work of creation, it began to move, and the creatures which were to constitute the future world were formed ...'.[49]

Among other conceptions of God in the Egyptian texts, we find that God is hidden and unknowable: 'thou art unknown and canst not be searched out ...';[50] that God has innumerable aspects: 'O thou mighty one of myriad forms and aspects ...';[51] that God is infinite and eternal: '... God is the eternal One, He is eternal and infinite and endureth forever ...';[52] that God is omnipotent: 'O thou art the mighty one of victories, thou art the power of all powers ...'.[53] In fact, most of the concepts of God prevalent in the foremost religions of the world can be found in ancient Egyptian religion. It is certainly not to the Greeks or to Judaism that we owe their origination. These concepts of God exist in African religion today. These concepts seem somehow universal to the religions of man and womankind and appear to arise by the very nature of our thinking and reflection upon our existence in the world.

1.
DISCERNING OPPOSITES: THE NOUMENAL AND THE PHENOMENAL

The African principle of opposites leads us to a duality at the foundation of nature in which there are two opposing aspects that are also complementary: the noumenal and phenomenal. The phenomenal refers to objects, which possess the possibility of being experienced either by the senses or as conceptions of the imagination. The noumenal (nothingness or the void) does not refer to any objects of experience and can neither be conceived by the senses nor conceived by the imagination. In the philosophies of various African peoples it is believed that the universe is divisible into a visible part and an invisible part (Heaven and Earth). In the beginning, Heaven and Earth were one, but were later separated.[1] We find that in the beginning the joining of Heaven and Earth in ancient Egyptian religion is represented by the goddess Nut of the sky and her husband, the god Seb of the earth, mutually embraced in the act of procreation. Thereafter, the pair were separated by the god Shu to make way for all the things which would come into existence as a result of their union.[2] As in traditional African religion in general, procreation symbolises the creation of the universe. It is a concrete and simple representation of a profound philosophical theme. To explain this representation further, in the Egyptian creation account[3] the potential of the empty primeval void to contain all existent things may be seen as a longing for a void to fill itself or, conversely, for matter to come into being. It is perfectly symbolic, in each case, of sexual desire. Diop, in comparing Egyptian and Phoenician cosmologies as replicas of each other, notes in Phoenician cosmology that Chephets is 'the Desire which is the origin of all creation'.[4] Chephets represents the union of the fundamental duality. Thus, by comparison, the ground (that is, the *conceptual* ground) of all existence is not the void by itself (the noumenal) or matter by itself (the phenomenal), but the interacting duality. In the beginning, the void is not alone absolutely; for it contained within itself the potential for everything to come into being. The interaction might be understood as the divine intelligence creating, in the form of pure thought, that which was to come into being. It only remained for this thought to be spoken as the Divine Word and hence initiate the momentum of creation.

Fig. 5 The Separation of Heaven (Goddess Nut) and Earth (God Seb). Shu (god of air and light), portrayed as the Ka (in hieroglyphs), and together with his assistants, part the deities of the earth and the sky to make way for everything which is to come into existence as a result of their sexual union.

European anthropologists have in the past been ignorant of the function of myth in African thought. Coupled with this the African mind was judged incapable of abstract or theoretical thinking and only able to form thoughts about the concrete. Consequently, on the basis of this racist and naive conception of the African mind, they lead themselves to see African myth, not as a medium or means of conveying any knowledge or wisdom; but as meaningless fantasy. Myth is an art form, and like all African art it is a medium through which ideas are communicated – myths are not created for their own sake just as art does not exist for it's own sake.

Some African authors have attempted to explain the function of myth in both traditional and ancient thought. Mbiti explains that in traditional African thought, 'A myth is a means of explaining some actual or imaginary reality which is not adequately understood and so cannot be explained through normal description. Myths do not have to be taken literally, since they are not synonymous with the facts. They are intended to communicate and form the basis for a working explanation about something'.[5] Egyptian myth has been misunderstood in the same way. Nobles explains that in ancient African thought, 'The importance of mythology is of course that it is a form of documentation which transcends the human record in as much as it states truth rather than fact. Myth can be considered a form of reasoning and record keeping which goes beyond reasoning and record keeping by providing an implicit guide for bringing about the fulfilment of the truth it proclaims. Myth connects the invisible order with the visible order.

'Myth is therefore the form in which the experience of a people has become conscious and as such should be viewed as a carefully constructed symbolic cloak for their abstract thought'.[6]

We might not fail to see that in African thought there is more than one level of understanding; abstract ideas are often represented on another level by the simple and concrete. Among the Dogon of Mali, only initiates of the priesthood are allowed access to 'deep knowledge'; otherwise, enquirers are given 'simple knowledge'.[7] The most obvious example in ancient African cosmology of a case where more than one level of meaning exists is in the account of the creation where the abstract conception of duality (either boundless water or void, and matter) is represented and concretised by the mythical sexual union of Nut, the goddess of the sky, and Seb, god of the earth.

At this point we delve into a more theoretical discourse on the duality. It would not seem to make sense to talk of the noumenal world (the void) directly; for it is intangible and unknowable. Since the noumenal world is the opposite of the phenomenal, we shall speak of it indirectly by reference to the phenomenal (i.e., the world of everyday experience). The phenomenal or the world possesses three essential attributes:[8]

Finiteness: Everything in the world is finite in every respect; i.e., every object is of limited size, weight, life-span, etc.

Discontinuity: Everything in the world is physically discontinuous in every respect. This is closely related to the property of being finite; there is a limit to every physical property of an object, i.e., nothing is infinitely long, smooth, dense, etc.

Entity: Everything in the world is an entity; i.e., all objects exist in time and space.

It is through the negation of these essential attributes of the world that we come to intuit the noumenal world of the void. If we negate finiteness, discontinuity and entity we arrive at infinity, continuity and non-entity. These are the conceptual attributes[9] of the void; i.e., they are not attributes of anything knowable or subject to experience. We may note how these very abstract ideas are conceived of and symbolised in ancient and traditional African thought. This trinity of concepts, infinity, continuity and non-entity may be represented by a single African religious symbol: the circle. Mbiti notes that in traditional African religions the circle is the symbol of both the infinity and continuity of the universe.[10] It had the same significance for the ancient Egyptians; and we note that both in traditional and ancient religions of Africa the circular symbol is formed by a snake with its tail in its mouth.[11] To complete this tri-lateral representation we also note that the circle is the symbol of the number zero, the numeric expression of non-entity. However, we only need note in relation to our discussion of the circle as a religious symbol, that it can be seen as trilaterally signifying infinity, continuity and non-entity, the negations of the world's trinity of essential attributes. A further symbol is synthesized out of the combination of the circle and the essential trinity: that of the triangle within the circle. Now, one who is sceptical may say this is another in a chain of coincidences; but according to Churchward the triangle or pyramid within the circle is also a religious symbol of ancient Africa.[12]

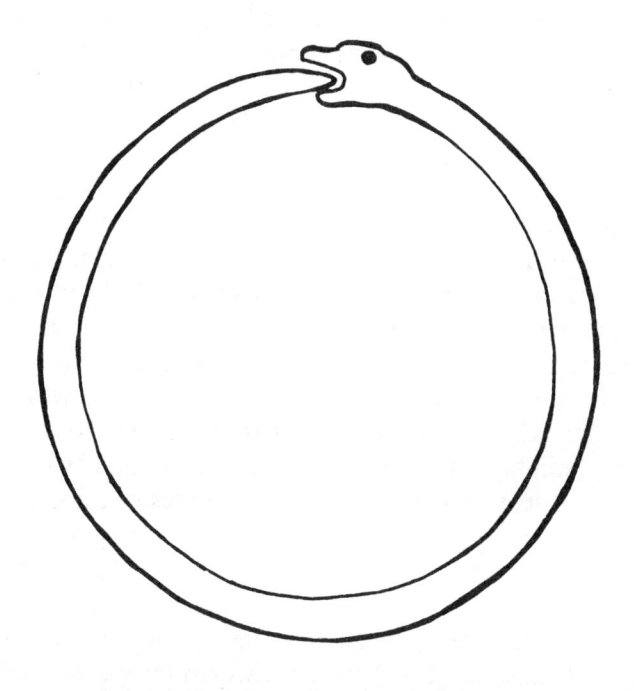

Fig. 6 Circle formed by Serpent with Tail in its Mouth.
This is the most fundamental mystical symbol of ancient and traditional Africa signifying infinity, continuity and the void (nothingness). These are the opposites of the three most fundamental attributes of matter: finiteness, discontinuity and 'thingness' (that is, the quality of existing in space and time).

It is, to say the least, odd for us to talk of the noumenal world as possessing 'attributes'. But these are obviously not attributes in any physical or tangible sense – only a conceptual one. They are a convenience, means by which we represent the noumenal, which defies description, in terms of the phenomenal which is available to it. We do this by representing the noumenal as the opposite of the phenomenal: the noumenal is *not* finite (i.e., it is infinite); the noumenal is *not* a discontinuity (i.e., it is a continuity); the noumenal is not an entity (i.e., it is a non-entity). Outside of this form of representation we cannot, in speaking of the noumenal, sensibly speak of what it *is*, but only what it *is not*. Infinity, continuity and non-entity shall be called noumena. All are alike references to the formlessness that is the void. In contrast, finiteness, discontinuity and non-entity all imply the form of the material world. When these diametrically opposite concepts are associated to form a single concept they always produce a paradox but also a synthesis. This rule from hereon will be referred to as the Principle of Interaction of Opposites.

The knowledge of the noumenal, we will recall, is gained by intuition through the negation of the fundamental attributes we ascribe to the phenomenal or ordinary world. What is meant precisely by intuition therefore needs to be clarified before proceeding further. Intuition is closely connected to emotional sense or feeling.[13] It is a form of immediate knowledge, a means by which knowledge is gained without recourse to reason. It might be argued that the act of discerning an opposite is an act of reason; but the ability to recognise an opposite by the rational process of negation does not precede the knowledge of its existence. One might, for instance, recognise the concept of the infinite as the opposite of the finite; but because each of these two terms cannot exist alone meaningfully without the other, they must therefore both already exist independent of any act of rational negation or discerning of opposites. We see from this that our concepts of finitude and infinitude are given to us through intuition. It could be contended that two opposing concepts are derived from experience if they are both applicable to experience; for instance, light – dark, female – male, long – short are opposites given in our experience. However, finitude – infinitude are not concepts which are both applicable to experience and although reason may be used to infer one from the other (that is, the infinite from the finite), this is not so much the use of reason to create a new concept as to confirm the existence of one we already possess, independent of reason.

2.
THE IDEAS

NATURE OF THE IDEAS

The essence of life is contradiction (not necessarily of the logical kind) and this is manifested in every field of human knowledge as an ideal which is a paradoxical union, yet at the same time a harmonious synthesis of opposites. In other words the essence of life is to be found in ideals created by the union of opposites. However, these opposites are compatible by the very fact that nature puts them together.

To concretise what has been said above we might say more specifically that contradiction is the essence of the relationship between people, between people and things, and between things. In the most plain example of the first case, true love between two people must involve a mutual respect of each other's freedom, yet love is at the same time a form of possession in the sense that one desires a hold on the other person's affections. To give an example of the second case, the addict (whether addicted to tobacco, or alcohol or any other substance) who wishes to break his addiction experiences an inner conflict between the desire to be free of the substance and the desire to experience its effects. In an example of the third case we look at the idea of space, which is really a system of relations between objects. Consider two objects which are some distance apart. We would suppose that the space between these objects can be halved; and that this halved space can also be halved; and that halved space can also be halved, etc. The space between the two objects can be halved indefinitely, an infinite number of times (we might say). Hence if the space between these objects is infinitely divisible there must be an infinite number of positions that an object could occupy within this finite space between the two objects. Therefore, if one of these objects was to move towards the other it would have to pass through an infinite number of positions to reach it. Now, since it takes a finite amount of time (however small this may be) for the object to move from one of these positions to the next it must, surely, be impossible for the object to traverse this infinite number of positions in a finite time. Yet this is a miracle we see happening all the time![1]

Thus we see that in everyday life contradiction underlies all of the relationships we experience about us. Our ideals are derived from the ordinary things we experience and they similarly manifest contradictions. The particular kind of ideal of which we speak in this chapter is called the Idea. The Ideas are unattainable ideals which have their use in urging us to strive towards moral, aesthetic and technical perfection. In presenting themselves as unreachable absolutes they induce us towards progress (of a relative sort). The term *absolute* here, refers to the ideal and unreachable nature of the Idea. It involves the ideal notions of, for instance, infallibility, infinity, permanence and total perfection which do not apply to worldly experience.

Accordingly, there are three forms of the Idea: the theoretical ideas which relate to thought (especially scientific thought); the practical Ideas which relate to action (especially moral action) and the aesthetic Ideas which relate to feeling (sensation and emotion) and are aspired towards through artistic expression. The theoretical Ideas have a legitimate use in giving consistency to thought; the practical Ideas, in giving purpose to action. The aesthetic Ideas might appear not to have any legitimate use; but art in Africa does not exist for art's sake. To understand this we have to examine the role of the arts in African society, and view the society as if it were an individual human being. African art may be thought of as the personality of the society as a whole, which is constituted of both temperament (in the case relating mainly to emotional expression) and intellect embodying the historical memory of the society as well as its conceptions of nature and the role of human beings within nature. Furthermore, African art serves to manifest and concretise the invisible spirit world.

One characteristic of the Idea is that it is paradoxical. This is due to our being disposed to seeing the Idea either from the point of view of reason or from the point of view of our intuition. It is seeing the Idea from two aspects which sometimes appear contradictory that gives rise to the paradox.

We deal with the Idea systematically; no claim is made to the presentation of all the Ideas here, but those presented should suffice as examples of their general nature and function in human knowledge. Certain Ideas are obviously very closely related and they have been grouped and discussed together. The discussion of each idea attempts to give a historical background as well as a description of its nature.

An important feature to note is that each branch of human knowledge has a related ideal, and therefore an Idea. We encounter the Idea of Supreme Personal Being in religion, the Idea of an Immortal or Permanent Self in religion and psychology, the Idea of Permanent Substance in physical science, the Idea of Infinite Number in Mathematics, the Idea of Absolute Good in religion and ethics, among others.

THE THEORETICAL IDEAS

It has been noted that the Ideas are paradoxical by nature. In the instance of the theoretical Ideas which are applicable to science this paradox arises as a result of associating the opposite types of notions, noumena (in the form of one or more of the notions, infinity, continuity and non-entity) and phenomena (in the form of a concept developed from experience) into a single concept. It is only with respect to the rather more rigidly definable theoretical Ideas that the earlier mentioned principle of interaction of opposites can be tested. Generally speaking, whatever the form of the Idea, when we take concepts derived from our experience and suppose them to still apply beyond what is humanly experiencable we will produce paradoxes. A couple of examples of theoretical Ideas readily come to mind. The Idea of a personal God (i.e., God in a human form) combines the empirical concept of a person with that of infinity in the sense that God is all-powerful; with that of continuity, in the sense that God is everywhere (omnipresent); and with that of non-entity, in the sense that God is invisible and exists in neither space nor time. In this Idea the concept of person, which is empirical (i.e., derived from experience), is clearly supposed applicable beyond the realm of human experience. Taking another theoretical example, the Idea of Absolute Truth takes many forms, one of which is that of a perfect physical measurement. It is impossible, for instance, to draw or construct an absolutely perfect circle – there will always be some degree of error. Consequently, every physical circle we construct or draw is an approximation to this Idea of a perfect circle. In this Idea, the conception of the physically constructed circle we find in experience is associated with the concept of the infinite in the sense that if this circle is to be perfect, it must be seen to represent the last in an infinite series of approximations to the Absolute Truth; and also the concept of continuity, in the sense that this physically constructed circle would have an absence of imperfections. Obviously this kind of perfection lies beyond experience and the result is a paradox when it is supposed that a perfect circle can exist physically.

The Idea of the Infinite Number

The notion of infinite number could never have had any sound mathematical basis without the so-called Pythagoras Theorem. This theorem is misnamed because it is widely agreed that it was known to the ancient Mesopotamians 2000 years before Pythagoras.[2] Furthermore, the theorem is implied both by Egyptian problems presented in a papyrus dating about 2000 B.C. and also the Egyptian use of the double remen as a unit of measure.[3] Many authors attest to Pythagoras learning his mathematics in Egypt. Warburton maintains that he studied for 20 years in Egypt and only set out his theorems on his return to Greece.[4] In school children are taught that Pythagoras was the father of mathematics, but Aristotle himself says: '… in Egypt mathematical sciences first commenced …'[5] and in Plato's *Phaidros* Socrates declares that Thoth, the Egyptian god of wisdom '… invented numbers and arithmetic and geometry … and most important of all letters…'.[6]

The Pythagoras Theorem is at the foundation of all modern

Fig7. The God Thoth.
The inventor of the arts and sciences and male counterpart of Maat. He is sometimes identified with the Egyptian Sage Hermes Trismegistus.

pure mathematics. For the theorem leads to the proof of the existence of irrational numbers (i.e., numbers which cannot be expressed as fractions and which have endless decimal arrays such as square root of 2 = 1.414213562 ... etc.), which in turn led to Cantor's proof of the existence of infinite (or transfinite) numbers which revolutionised mathematics in the western world. It seems as if the body of modern mathematics is a pyramid standing on its apex. Cantor himself admitted: 'One can without qualification say that the transfinite numbers stand or fall with the infinite irrationals ...'.[7]

Until this day there is a controversy surrounding the existence of the Infinite Number, which highlights the paradoxical nature of the Idea.[8] Amongst exponents against the existence of an Infinite Number were the philosophers Kant and Leibnitz. However the existence of infinite numbers (not just one infinite number!) is generally accepted in western mathematical circles following the work of Georg Cantor in the late 19th century. However, ever since this theory became widely accepted there have been, and still are, mathematicians who do not agree with the notion of the Infinite Number from a philosophical viewpoint. Among these was the greatly respected Poincare. Interestingly, following the work of Godel (1930),[9] it seems we can never ever know for certain which school of thought is correct. Consequently, neither side can absolutely refute the other.

The subject of the Infinite Number has been the cause of the most serious schism in western mathematics since it began. The two philosophical camps involved have been called *existentialist* and *constructivist*. An existentialist mathematician is one who believes that a number does not have to be exhibitable in order for its existence to be proven; whereas the constructivist believes that the only numbers which can be said to exist are those which can be exhibited (that is, constructed or shown, intuitively, to exist).

One can easily demonstrate the difference between the existentialist and constructivist philosophies by examining an example given by Bertrand Russel. Russel attempts to show the existence of the Infinite Number and his argument is existentialist. By turning Russel's argument on its head we can arrive at a constructivist case against the existence of an Infinite Number. Russel argues as follows:

> Cantor also overcame the longstanding logical puzzles about infinite numbers. Take the series of whole numbers from 1 onwards; how many of them are there? Clearly the number is not finite. Up to a thousand, there are a thousand numbers; up to a million, a million. Whatever finite number you mention, there are evidently more numbers than that, because from 1 up to the number in question there are just that number of numbers, and then there are others that are greater. The number of finite whole numbers must therefore be *an infinite number*.[10] (Emphasis mine)

The crux of the controversy is this: can the aggregate of finite whole numbers be described by a single number? The existentialists say it can and that the number which describes it is an Infinite Number. The constructivists say there is no single number which can describe the aggregate of finite whole numbers. Who is right?

I believe that because of the essentially paradoxical nature of the Idea (of which Infinite Number is an example), the controversy will remain unsettled. The Infinite Number controversy is analogous to an age old controversy surrounding another Idea; that of the Supreme Being. The arguments used by the contesting camps are precisely the same. There are those that say God does not exist because there is no visible proof. Others say that the proof lies in the nature of those things which are visible in the same way that existentialist mathematicians argue that the proof of the Infinite Number lies in the nature of the finite numbers.

Having these things in mind we proceed to turn Russel's example on its head. Take the series of whole numbers from one onwards. The series is endless; but clearly, all the numbers in the series are finite. Whatever number you mention there are others beyond it that are greater, but these others are finite. If there is an Infinite Number, where is it? It evidently does not appear in sequence. There can, therefore, be no Infinite Number because all of the numbers are finite.

The point made in the above argument is not that there do not exist infinite series, only that there are no such things as infinite numbers. The existentialist argument assumes that the series of whole numbers has only *one* total which describes the entire series, and that this total is infinite. The constructivist (or finitist) position put forward is that the series of finite whole numbers is described not by one, but by many totals, all of which are finite. Indeed, the notion of infinity (it is contended here) has nothing to do with the concept of number and these two ideas are arrived at by quite separate channels. Whereas numbers are concepts we construct through a logical step-by-step process of our *reason*; infinity is a notion we arrive at through our *intuition*; for we find no evidence of the infinite in the entire sequence of natural numbers, yet we still arrive at the idea. We note that the addition of one finite number to another will only produce a further finite number.

It is evident that when the noumenal notion of *infinity* is associated with the phenomenal concept of *number*, the result is a paradoxical Idea which is at the same time a synthesis of the opposites, *infinity* and *finiteness*. The constructivist or finitist would argue that the essence of a number is that it is finite.

The above inversion of Russel's argument for the existence of the Infinite Number is not in any way intended as a formal proof. The inversion, as well as Russel's argument itself, suffers from a circularity in that they would both appear, in some way, to quietly assume what they are setting out to prove. By asking the question 'how many?' Russel already assumes that the series of whole numbers can be counted and has one total; whilst by concluding there can be 'no Infinite Number because all of the numbers are finite' the inversion of his argument assumes that the only type of numbers which can exist are finite. These arguments, although flawed, serve to show the difference between existentialist and constructivist approaches, as well as the paradoxical nature of the Idea.

The Ideas of Absolute Empirical Truth, Absolute Natural Law and Unfailing Causation

Fig. 8 The Goddess Maat.
She personified righteousness, truth and justice and the operation of natural and moral law. She is the female counterpart of Thoth.

As might be expected, in the light of their contact with the ancient Egyptians, the ancient Greek's meaning of justice was very similar to the Egyptian's concept of *Maat*. We will recall that this concept, personified by the goddess Maat, signifies justice, truth and righteousness and possesses both a physical and moral significance especially in terms of the notion of justice, which in the physical aspect means that every effect has a cause, whilst in the ethical or moral sense means that every action has a result which is in its likeness, good or bad – the balance is always redressed. Of the Greek idea Russel says:

> The idea of justice, both cosmic and human, played a part in Greek religion and philosophy which is not altogether easy for a modern to understand; ... there is a kind of necessity or natural law which perpetually redresses the balance.[12]

It seems that the spirit of *Maat* has not been lost in the recesses of African consciousness; for traditional African thought still readily makes the connection between the notions of truth, natural law and justice.[13] Maat, therefore, has both a moral and physical significance which embodies the theoretical Ideas of Absolute Truth, Absolute Natural Law and unfailing Causation.[14] In contrast, modern Western science and belief does not seem to possess any comparable concept embodying both science and ethics in parallel. This might suggest the concept never belonged to Western thought in the first place; since it has not survived in any form.

The nature of the above Ideas is well described by the history of Western science. In the past Western science has supposed the existence of absolute truths in the form of absolute natural laws. Newton's Laws of Gravitation like the laws of Galileo and Copernicus before him, were largely thought to be absolute and eternal until the 19th century, when scientists could not make it account for the strange orbit of planet Mercury around the sun.[15] No theory could fully account for this until the arrival of Einstein's General Theory of Relativity. Scientists then abandoned their belief in the absolute nature of Newton's law, which was to some degree, only replaced by the idea that a truly absolute natural law had been found in the theory of relativity. Today scientists can see that even Einstein's theory has its limits,[16] and the trend is not in favour of there being Absolute Empirical Truths, Absolute Natural Laws and, following from the latter, Unfailing Causation (i.e., the trend does not favour the belief that every effect has a cause in accordance with natural law).

Truth, defined as a correspondence between statement and fact is a fundamental concept of empirical science. These Ideas, in accordance with this definition of truth entail and imply the completion of an infinite series of correspondences between scientific statement and fact. But in science these Ideas have to be supposed though no evidence of their reality exists in experience. They are paradoxes arising from the joining of the intuitive notion of infinity with the empirical concept of truth.

Karl Popper noted that the falsification of scientific theory is often more important than its verification. By his argument science progresses not by revealing absolute truths but by discarding outmoded ones.[17] Science evidently survives without revealing any absolute truths (and therefore any absolute natural laws) – it experiences no difficulty in working with mere approximate truths – but in order to maintain its consistency it must suppose that these approximate truths tend towards some absolute. For instance, if I wish to measure the length of an object there are various ways of doing so, some more accurate than others. It is impossible to measure anything without some degree of error, and all measurements will be approximations (some better than others); but approximations to what? We cannot avoid supposing that the object possesses *one* absolute and true length; but this length can't possibly be measured. It seems that the length of the object represents an absolute truth we are forced to suppose exists, but which gives no evidence of existing in time and space (an evident paradox). We recall from the introduction to this part, that the Egyptians referred to the Ideas as forms (aru), and in the *Book of the Dead* these are said not to exist in time and space but in heaven: 'Thou art crowned with a heavenly form the Only One provided (with all things)'.

The Ideas of the Continuity of Space and Time

From the African point of view space and time are conceived as being constituted solely of objects and events respectively,[18] as opposed to being certain kinds of ethereal containers as Western science conceives them. Western science idealizes space and time as perfect continuities. Africans do believe in a continuity, but this permeates all things and pervades all the universe, as opposed to merely enveloping or containing all things. This all-pervading continuity underlies space and time themselves and should not be confused with them.[19]

There is nothing wrong in Western science idealizing space and time as being continuities or uniformities. The idealization is made legitimate by the simple fact that it facilitates the application of science to nature. However, from a philosophic viewpoint, the scientist should forever be aware that these ideal conceptions are merely convenient tools of mathematics and physics and cannot absolutely represent things as they really are.

The Idea of Permanent Substance

Fig. 9 Shabaka Stone (British Museum).
The stone is dated 700 B.C. and has written into it the Memphite Theology, the religion, cosmology and philosophy of the ancient Africans of Egypt.

Fig. 10 The Goddess Hathor – Often taken to represent energy.

Where do our notions of permanent indivisible substance derive from? As is characteristic of all the Ideas, it results from applying a concept derived from experience beyond the realm of experience. Substance as related to our experience of enduring and tangible matter is a concept derived from our experience. When this substance is thought of as enduring eternally, we have the Idea. Evidently, eternity lies beyond the realm of experience.

Before the 19th century it had been the general belief that the atom was the fundamental and indivisible unit of matter. Most would attribute the origin of this conception to the ancient Greeks Leucippus and Democritus; but according to James the earliest text in which we find the allusion to the atom is the Memphite Theology,[20] an inscription on the Shabaka Stone kept in the British Museum and containing the religion, cosmology and philosophy of the ancient Africans. The stone is dated at 700 B.C.

In modern times, however, Rutherford's discovery of the electron in the 19th century has opened up a whole new world beyond the atom. Today there are not only found to be electrons, but a group of some thirty-odd relatively stable atomic particles called 'strange particles'. These have no exact shape, size, location, mass or speed; they incessantly disappear, evaporating into waves of energy at some point in their motion, reforming again into particles at some other location.[21] The point which it has been attempted to illustrate is that in what is seemingly a chaotic flux of events, there is really nothing underlying which is identifiable as substance. Man and woman's search for the permanent substance would therefore appear to have been so far in vain. Is there hope such a substance will be found in the future?

Despite perennial disappointment it is never long before human faith is revived and the search resumed with renewed vitality. The belief in a permanent substance is so recurrent we may well ask whether this Idea is necessary to our understanding of reality. Although man and woman have come back again and again to search for the permanent substance, the historical trend of science has not been in favour of its existence.

But for the world to be intelligible, we must suppose it to

have some degree of fixity or permanence in time. It would seem that science's most permanent of substances today is energy; yet this is an abstraction, an Idea of permanence which human beings create to make the world more readily understandable. Energy is the Life Force born of the interaction of the fundamental duality in African religions. The interaction of Pemba and Faro spells both the conservation and the change associated with the energy concept of modern science.[22] Although energy, from the viewpoint of African religions, is manifested in many forms its quantity in nature is always preserved.

The Idea of Permanent Self (The Soul and Immortality)
The doctrines of the soul and immortality are to be found in the Egyptian *Book of Coming Forth By Day (Egyptian Book of the Dead)*: 'I am Shu the god of unformed matter. My soul is God, my soul is eternity'.[23]

Traditional and ancient African (Egyptian) religions have in common the belief that the person is made up of physical and spiritual entities. Mbiti identifies some of the traditional African entities as 'soul, life, breath, shadow or double'[24] and he acknowledges that there are others and that this is an area of African belief which requires further research.[25] One might wish to compare these with the nine entities of the ancient Egyptians given by Budge: Ka or double, Ba or soul, Ab or heart, Khu or intelligence, Khaibit or shadow, Sekhem or form, Ren or name, Khat or physical body, Sahu or spiritual body.[26] These themselves are apparently not sufficiently understood. Confusion seems to exist over the meanings of Ba and Ka. Here we take the Ka to be the personality or the abstraction of individuality made up by the unique flux of a person's thoughts, sensations, and emotions. The Ba is taken to be the soul or life-force of the individual. The Khat or Jet as it is sometimes called is the physical body. These three definitions are given by most authors. They are the three aspects of the self with which we shall be most concerned. The Khat and the Ka are really aspects of the physical self; whilst the Ba is the immaterial or transcendent self.

The Ba is a paradoxical Idea. Beyond the experience of the

body and of thoughts, sensations and emotions, it would seem there is nothing else. Yet, in agreement with a Kantian theory, this immaterial self (which Kant called the 'I think') *must* be supposed, and is a concept which must accompany every experience of the senses for coherent experience to be possible.[27] If it did not, one could have no sense of self identity and separateness from the object of experience; in every situation of perception there must be an 'I' apart and distinct from 'the-object-which-I-perceive'. This is fundamental to perception, which first of all requires the awareness that 'something is there';[28] but this cannot be possible if one cannot in the first instance distinguish the self (as subject) from that 'something' (as object). The immaterial self is a paradoxical Idea in the sense which Kant alludes to.[29] Though the soul or immaterial self cannot be an object of experience (since it is non-physical) it is supposed as having a location in space, i.e., in a human body. We recall from the last chapter that anything which exists in space and time must possess at least the possibility of being experienced by the senses; but a non-physical substance (a paradoxical term in itself) cannot possess this possibility.[30]

An important aspect which traditional African religions seem to have retained from their ancient Egyptian roots is the belief in immortality. In traditional African religions there are in general two kinds: collective immortality and personal immortality. We shall first of all deal with the former, for this is the other aspect of the Idea of Permanent Self. Out of interest we shall also say a few words about the latter. The traditional and ancient conceptions of the spirit are closely associated with breathing, since the breath is taken to be the basis of life; when this has gone life ceases. When the spirit leaves the body at death it somehow maintains its individuality, according to certain authors.[31] But a version in which the spirit loses its individuality or personality is quite consistent. The immaterial self or soul must surely be separate from one's thoughts, feelings, emotions and sensations, simply because it cannot be identified as being any one of these phenomena and because we are able to observe and reflect upon these as if we existed apart from them. This self is not an object of experience, so in what sense can it be unique and maintain an individuality? Uniqueness and individuality derives from the body or physiology of the individual. How the spirit is able to maintain this individuality is not clear; although this is not by the inhabitance of another body.[32] According to the ancient Egyptian account, at death the spirit is freed from the finiteness of the body to become one with the Supreme Consciousness (or All-Pervading Spirit).[33] But this All-Pervading Spirit possesses no worldly attributes and in order for the individual spirit to merge and become one with this Spirit it would have to lose its individuality. Retaining the individuality might be seen as equivalent to the case in Eastern religion where the retention of karma causes rebirth or reincarnation; only when all karma is eliminated is the spirit then freed from rebirth to become one with the Supreme Consciousness. To retain individuality is to be bound to the body; not until this individuality is lost can the spirit be free to merge with the Supreme Consciousness or All-Pervading Spirit. It is possible that Asian and ancient African religions are related in this sense and that the retention of individuality after death in ancient Africa is not a must, but like Asian religions (specifically Hinduism and Buddhism) it depends on the extent to which the individual has lead a virtuous life.

It is the Ba, the immaterial self which possesses absolute immortality. We have already noted the proclamation made in the Egyptian *Book of the Dead*: 'My soul is God, my soul is eternity'. This brings to light not only a resemblance between ancient and traditional African thought, but also between African and Eastern religious thought (specifically Hindu and Buddhist thought). Mbiti notes that in Africa God is 'outside and beyond his creation. On the other hand he is personally involved in his creation, so that it is not outside of him or his reach. God is simultaneously transcendent and immanent, a balanced understanding of these two is necessary in our discussion of African conceptions of God'.[34] Here the immanence of God rests in the Ba or soul whereas the transcendence rests in the void or All-Pervading Spirit. This is identical with the Hindu concept of Brahman. Brahman is '... God, the Ultimate, understood to be without attributes ... God is not in the image of man, nor can it be described by any human words or categories of thought. Brahman is not divided among beings, but standing in them as though divided, maintaining all beings ... seated in the hearts of all'.[35]

Personal immortality, that which is linked to reverence for our ancestors, consists in the memory of the deceased. The deceased is thought to live on in the memories of family, friends, acquaintances, etc. Remembrance by posterity is either by virtue of deeds alone or name alone. When there are none left living who remember the deceased, personal immortality is lost and the deceased becomes 'completely dead'.[36] The ancient Egyptians attached the same importance to the preservation of the name as do traditional Africans. Blotting out of the name was also thought to destroy the deceased.[37]

The Idea of the Personal Supreme Being

We have already noted the existence of monotheism in Egypt and its resurgence in the era of Moses and the Pharaoh Akhenaton. For as far back as history is able to record man and woman have possessed the concept of one Supreme God who has always been personalised or conceived in the human image. However, because the Supreme God has always been conceived in abstract terms as immaterial, unknowable and infinite, the Idea becomes paradoxical as a result of the fusion of these abstract and concrete conceptions. We find that since we are ascribing the qualities of a human being, which are necessarily limited and lacking perfection to that which is unlimited and unlacking in perfection, paradox must result.

The paradoxical nature of this Idea, however, does not invalidate its use. Like all other Ideas, it is adopted as a matter of convenience by the user. For many this Idea is able to give both a consistency and purpose to life and is in this sense necessary. By this definition of use the Idea is both theoretical and practical. It is theoretical in providing some with a cosmological explanation of the world; through God one may find an acceptable explanation of how the world came to be. It is practical in providing a moral standard for some by which they are able to live; God conceived as the ultimate keeper of the moral law provides a sanction of punishment which inspires self-discipline and virtue in some. For some, it is not enough to seek strength only within themselves in conditions of adversity; through the use of the Idea one is able to invoke the 'presence' of an all-powerful guardian, and promote one's sense of security. For others there is faith in the endless potential of the self for strength and resolve precluding the need to invoke the Idea of a separate Supreme Being. In this instance it is the Idea of the Self which replaces the Idea of an external Supreme Being; both serve the same function in facilitating the art of living and neither Idea is more real than the other. Inevitably, a futile contest has always taken place between the believer and non-believer in which one must prove the belief of the other to be mistaken. But since the existence of God cannot be either proven or refuted by reason, as Kant has shown,[38] the result of such controversy has always been fruitless. Objectively speaking, atheism and theism are equally valid, for there exists no triumphant argument for or against either position. Subjectively, each person makes a choice related to her/his particular disposition to be a believer or non-believer.

Nevertheless, the Idea is not a static and independent reality, but one which is realised by its use. For instance, a scientific concept like the law of conservation of energy is not really thought as having an independent existence outside the minds of human beings, but through its application it is continually confirmed to be true; it is therefore realised through its usage. In the same way, the Idea is a reality confirmed only by its use. This is consistent with the notion of faith in world religions, where it is held that God will not help man and woman until they are able to exercise faith and help themselves. True faith or belief is shown through action and faith in God is no more than the whole-hearted application of the Idea. This inevitably leads to results: many will have witnessed the energy that belief in the Idea is able to release in zealous individuals.

All this does not deny or affirm the unconditional and independent existence of a God per se. It does, however, deny the unconditional and independent existence of a *personal* God in the same way that the unconditional and independent existence of all other Ideas is denied – the Ideas cannot exist independent of the human mind. The unconditional and independent existence of an *impersonal* God remains at the same time unprovable and irrefutable. This God is nature or the world as a whole. This God possesses no attributes, let alone those human ones man ascribes to it such as listening, punishing, guarding, showing mercy, etc. In short, the human being through the creation of the Idea, moulds the concept of God into a human image. In this way God becomes more reachable and understandable. A God which has an unconditional existence independent of human beings would have to be neither good nor evil, neither merciful nor merciless; such a God would be indifferent and exist solely as the ground of reality.

THE PRACTICAL IDEAS

Absolute Good, Absolute Moral Law, Unfailing Will

To the theoretical Ideas of Absolute Truth, Absolute Natural Law and Unfailing Causation there correspond the practical Ideas of Absolute Good, Absolute Moral Law and Unfailing Will. Both groups of Ideas clearly reveal the parallel that exists between ethics and physical science. This parallel is embodied in the ancient Egyptian concept of Maat, which we will remember signified both physical and ethical truth, justice and righteousness.

We have seen that the Idea of a Personal Supreme Being has both a theoretical and a practical aspect. In the practical aspect the Supreme Being provides an absolute moral standard as the essence of goodness. God is conceived as the Absolute Good. God is the author and the guardian of the moral law; He (She) is the personification of Absolute Moral Law, for His (Her) justice and righteousness are conceived as beyond dispute and as transcending the diversity of human opinion.

God, the Absolute Good, is the Idea towards which man and woman aspire in search of moral perfection, in quest of becoming god-like. To achieve the impossible and become god-like would require an absolute adherence to the moral law, an Unfailing Will, which, in typical character of the Idea, is paradoxical. This is because, in effect, one who abides unfailingly by the moral law is determined by it, so it would appear that the person no longer exercises the choice between good and evil; for he is, in effect, conditioned to do good by the very existence of an absolute moral standard and robbed of his freewill.

The Aesthetic Idea

The aesthetic Idea relates to art and one of the functions of African art is that of concretising the spiritual world. The concrete manifestation of the spiritual world in the physical world is a contradiction which is the essence of the aesthetic Idea. Many African artists working in the sixties were wrongly labelled as surrealists; for they were merely returning to their traditions, using art to manifest the subconscious.

It might be asked what relevance the aesthetic Idea has to our everyday lives. As human beings we all have hopes, dreams, aspirations. It is by means of our creativity that we transform these phantoms into realities. The world we create is never near as perfect as our wildest dreams, but it remains a better place for us having those dreams. Our dreams, hopes and aspirations for our world are our aesthetic Ideas.

3.
THE ARTS AND THE SCIENCES IN AFRICA

INTRODUCTION

In Africa the arts and sciences are interrelated. The traditional doctor, for example, recognises the therapeutic value of art. The reason why the arts and sciences in Africa are able to be interrelated in this way is partly due to the two-dimensional character of African science; for African science is not merely an objective material science. It is a science which recognises the existence of psychic forces or phenomena. Western science is now awakening to the existence of psychic phenomena through the formation of a new branch of psychology called para-psychology. Generally speaking, however, western science, by its nature, chooses only to deal with the physical or material world and does not recognise the existence of anything beyond this. As a result of this position the sciences of other cultures which do recognise forces of a psychic nature have been misnomered in the West as 'magic', as if these phenomena had no explicable cause.

The Western division of art and science as wholly dissimilar and incompatible bed mates is disadvantageous. They could both just as well be called sciences; for the arts are spiritual sciences which have to do with the resolution of conflicts and contradictions we subjectively experience within ourselves. George Thompson in his book *The Human Essence* describes the artist and the scientist as follows:

> The scientist and artist are both concerned to change the world – the one the external world of man's objective relations with nature, the other the internal world of his subjective relation with his fellow men. The scientist

discovers a contradiction in his consciousness of the external world and resolves it in a scientific hypothesis; the artist discovers a contradiction in his consciousness of the internal world and resolves it in a work of art. Both are creative acts.[1]

Thompson goes on to say that the scientist thus extends our knowledge of the external world; whereas the artist heightens our social awareness. He fails to note that the artist extends his knowledge of human nature through self knowledge together with social interaction. Thus science and art are not so dissimilar, only their subjects differ. Thompson goes on to say: 'This does not mean to say the two are independent of one another. The two worlds in which they do their special work are inseparable aspects of the social world in which they live and work together. Moreover, even in their special work the scientist cannot escape from the subject or the artist from the object'.[2]

One of the arguments used to make a case for the incompatible natures of science and art is based on the division between reason and emotion. It is popularly held that whereas art is purely emotional, science is purely rational and in a technological Western world reason is held to be superior to emotion as science is held to be superior to art. However, reason and emotion are both inseparable and essential elements of human nature. By the very fact that scientists and artists are human beings, scientific creativity and observation cannot be unemotional neither can artistic creativity and appreciation be wholly irrational. In scientific creativity the scientist, before he has totally conceived of his theory or explanation, only has a gut feeling that he is close to obtaining the solution to his problem. He then goes on to confirm that his *feeling* was correct or otherwise. In the case of the artist, when a person goes to watch a play or see a film or exhibition of artwork he cannot fully appreciate this without use of his rational faculties for the work of art has to make some kind of sense. Beyond the gut response elicited by a work of art there follows a stage in which the observer wishes to ascertain the *meaning* of the work before him or her.

In all this we must place pure mathematics in its proper place as being a spiritual science or art, not a material science. This is because investigations in pure mathematics tell us nothing about the external material world; rather they reveal the nature of woman and man, the ways in which we are naturally conditioned to think and to understand the world about us. Having said this, pure mathematics, in the following text is still dealt with under the topic of African science which is not universally acknowledged.

AFRICAN SCIENCE

Egyptian Science

It is generally not accepted that African people have made any contribution to the world of science. However, the pyramids, and in particular the Great Pyramid of Giza, provide abundant evidence of the highly advanced scientific and technological skills of ancient Africans. Till this day the building of the pyramids remains a mystery and even with today's technology such a task would require great skill and resources. Sir William Flinders Petrie, considered by Western archaeological circles as the father of modern scientific archaeology, noted that in order to cut building blocks used to construct the Great Pyramid a pressure of two tons would have to be placed on a drill. He speculated that the ancients must have used saws with teeth of hard jewels.[3]

The dimensions of the Great Pyramid appear to be loaded with highly advanced mathematical and astronomical information. Edme Francois Jomard, one of a collection of French savants who accompanied Napoleon on his 1798 expedition to Egypt, claimed that the sciences of geography and geodesy were immortalised in the construction of the Great Pyramid.[4] John Taylor, in the 19th century, claimed the pyramids were built to incorporate geometric and astronomical laws.[5] Numerous other authors such as Professor Piazzi Smyth, Astronomer Royal of Scotland and David Davidson in the late 18th and early 19th centuries respectively concluded that the building of the Great Pyramid must have required deep acquaintance with the workings of natural law. Davidson claims that it implies also knowledge of the specific gravity of the earth and the speed of light.[6]

Among concepts and entities of pure mathematics suggested by various authors as known to the ancient Africans are the number 'pi', the Pythagoras Theorem, the Golden Number and transcendental numbers. Modern mathematician Beatrice Lumpkin cites as proof of the Egyptian knowledge of *pi* to a greater accuracy than any approximation of ancient times, the fact that the perimeter of the base of the Great Pyramid of Giza divided by its height gives this value for *pi*.[7] Schwaller de Lubicz spent 15 years studying the Temple of Luxor and through his study of the dimensions of doorways in the temple amply demonstrated not only Egyptian familiarity with the Golden Number but also of its direct relation to the number *pi*.[8]

Most of the existing evidence for a highly developed ancient African mathematics rests in the Moscow Mathematical Papyrus. The late Dr. Cheikh Anta Diop noted among other things that the papyrus shows a diagrammatic representation of a transcendental number[9] as below:

Only in the 19th century was the existence of transcendental numbers proved by Georg Cantor.

Science or Magic?: The Cultural Relativity of Science

In the academic world, the cultural relativity of ethics is generally accepted (i.e., it is generally accepted that the rules of ethical behaviour vary from one society to another) but the cultural relativity of science is not so widely accepted. In the main introduction we noted the five fundamental tenets of western science. The first of these has served to reinforce the hegemony of western science and states that 'science is fundamentally culturally independent and universal'.

We might look at two definitions of science, one given by the Oxford Dictionary and the other by Hunter Adams III with the aid of the psychologist Wade Nobles. In the Oxford Dictionary science is 'knowledge arranged in an orderly manner, especially knowledge obtained by observation and testing of facts; pursuit of such knowledge'. It is also given to be the opposite to art. Adams, on the other hand, says that 'science – all science – be it the physical sciences, the social sciences or the spiritual sciences (and by the latter I mean music, art, philosophy/religion) is the search for unity or wholeness within or without all human experience. More explicitly, as theoretical psychologist Wade Nobles observes "science is the formal reconstruction or representation of a peoples set of systematic and cumulative ideas beliefs and knowledge (i.e., common sense) stemming from their culture". Thus science cannot always spring from a universal or culturally independent base. It must be consistent with the essentials of its peoples' common sense.'[10]

Thus Adams, with the help of Nobles, rejects the view that science is culturally universal. This belief has been maintained, preserving the Western monopoly on what we term 'science'. The science of all other cultures has instead been called 'magic', which is popularly understood to be almost the opposite of science. The magical world is not the world of causes and effects. It is instead the world of effects without explicable causes. In other words, it is in Western terms an impossible world. Things 'just happen' in the magical world. There are no valid principles involved, no system – only superstitious belief.

However, strong implications of the scientific nature of what is termed 'magic' come from the work of an English academic, Sir James Frazer. In his work, *The Golden Bough*, in trying to show that magic has nothing to do with science he has instead revealed the similarities. He admits that '... while science has this much in common with magic that both rest on a faith in order as the underlying principle of all things readers of this work will hardly need to be reminded that the order presupposed by magic differs widely from that which forms the basis of science. The difference flows naturally from the different modes in which the two orders have been reached. For whereas the order from which magic reckons is merely an extension, by false analogy, of the order in which ideas present themselves to our minds, the order laid down by science is derived from patient and exact observation of the phenomena themselves'.[11]

To counter Frazer's first claim that the orders presupposed by magic and science differ we shall shortly demonstrate this not to be the case; especially since the rudiments of Western science are to be found in the principles of 'magic'. To his second claim that 'magic', or rather, the science of Southern peoples has no basis in observation we need only ask how it is, for instance, that the Baka people of the Cameroun rain forest know that the mashed pulp of a certain tree, when soaked in the river will eventually cause the fish in it to come to the surface for air, making them easy to catch? The mashed pulp of the tree they use releases the chemical oestrogen in solution when soaked in the water. The oestrogen gums up the gills of the fish and forces them to come up to the water surface for air. For the Baka to go as far as bashing bits of a particular tree to pulp and to soak them in the river would presuppose them having knowledge of their environment which could only have been gained through long and patient observation.

Here Frazer has been blatantly unscientific in dismissing magic to be a pseudo-science based on false principles without having tested these principles (which he presents earlier in the same work). It is contended here that Frazer's distinction between magic and science is not at all helpful. Rather, it should be noted that whereas science explains how observed effects are linked to certain causes, or predicts the effects of certain events in a logical and rational manner; magical phenomena (as popularly conceived) cannot be explained in the same rational manner and would not appear to have physical causes. Indeed, magical phenomena are seen to be the product of a good or an evil will. We see that whereas scientific phenomena have physical causes, magical ones have psychic causes. This definition or distinction is valid only in the terms in which magic and science are popularly understood by westerners.

At this point we look at the fundamental principles of so-called 'magic' as identified by Frazer in *The Golden Bough*.

1. The Law of Similarity – that like produces like.

2. The Law of Contact – that things which have once been in contact with each other continue to act on each other at a distance after the physical contact has been severed.[12]

We may see that the principles of magic as discerned by Frazer are indeed the principles of a science by comparing them with Newton's laws of motion and looking at these principles of magic from a purely physical rather than psychic point of view:

(i) The resemblance between the Law of Similarity above and Newton's Third Law of Motion which states that *action and reaction are equal and opposite*, is quite plain to see.

(ii) Newton's First Law of Motion states that *everybody continues in its state of rest or uniform motion in a straight line unless acted upon by external forces*. This actually derives from an Aristotelian principle which says that: 'The moving body comes to a standstill when the force which pushes it along can no longer so act as to push it'.[13] If we compare the Law of Contact with Newton's First Law the resemblance is more easily seen through its Aristotelian predecessor. However, the scientific nature of the Law of Contact can be revealed by considering a concrete instance in which Newton's First Law applies. If we consider a moving object such as a billiard ball which collides with a second billiard ball at rest, this second ball will move some distance before coming to rest again. It would make sense to think of the second ball as remaining in motion due to the continued action of a force brought about by the contact of the first and the second balls. Thus the first ball may be conceived as acting on the second ball at a distance, after physical contact between them has been severed.

Whether one sees these principles of magic as valid or not; or as being identical, in some aspects, with Newton's laws or not, one can see from the comparisons made that they are scientific principles in as much as they leave themselves open to proof or disproof as well as being logically feasible. One could well imagine such laws being scientifically established in some alternative 'Aristotelian' system.

In reality, what we popularly term magic is an alternative form of science in which causes are both physical and psychic. Indeed, the physical and the psychic world cannot always be cleanly separated. Western science is now beginning to discover this with the introduction of parapsychology. Charles Finch observes that 'Even modern medicine concedes that as much as 60% of illness has a psychic base and indeed, the well-known "placebo" effect of modern pharmaco-medicine arises from this'.[14]

Janheinz Jahn, in speaking of the importance and power of the word in African medicine,[15] looks at the incantations which the traditional doctor uses with a secret extract of herbs to treat the patient. He notes that at times the patient was not even required to swallow the herbs. Instead, the patient might have been required to carry the hollow tooth of a beast under his arm. This kind of thing would have been dismissed by other ethnologists as the replacement of true medicine with 'hocus – pocus'. It would have been supposed that there was no relation between the traditional doctor's treatment and the disease, and that 'therefore the medicine was ineffective and the mysterious 'mumbo jumbo' nonsensical. Its only point was to conceal from the patient the incapacity of the physician'.[16] However, the 'placebo' experiments in America have shone a new light on the African traditional physicians so-called 'hocus – pocus' and 'mumbo jumbo'. Says Jahn:

> 'Placebo' is the name for a wholly indifferent substance, which contains no remedy but looks and tastes and is packaged like the medicine it is imitating. In these experiments the patient, without knowing it, is given the placebo instead of the medicine. ... The results established, for example, that 60% of all the people with headaches respond to a placebo and in 30 to 40 percent of the cases the pain can be relieved by a solution of common salt. Approximately the same number of asthmatics were relieved of their attack'.[17]

Jahn goes on to quote Professor Jores, director of the University clinic at Hamburg as saying:

> Even in the field of medicine, which is striving for objectivity and scientific accuracy, the magical effect plays an uncontrollable part which is frequently overlooked ... at least 40% of all individuals respond positively to a remedy no matter what it contains. ... The subtle compounding of many medicaments is probably 'magic' and without objective value. It is not an exaggeration to assert that the pharmaceutical industry is really manufacturing placebos on the grand style.[18]

Thus in Jahn's view, even in the west the restoration of health has a strong dependence on the personality of the physician and the faith of the patient. He concludes that 'In the light of African Philosophy all medicines are powerless by themselves and effective only in connection with the power of the word'.[19]

If we start with Western science as our frame of reference, it is not easy to show African beliefs to be a coherent system of thought, since the African system involves the psychic as well as the physical. What we understand as science in the Western world strictly confines itself to the physical and, on principle, the spiritual or psychic element plays no part (although modern views, especially in the field of medicine, are changing in regard to this). Western science will, for instance, explain *how* atoms behave and will exhaustively define and explain the motion of atoms; but it will not speak of what it is that causes the motion of the atoms in the first place. In African belief, which many authors have referred to as 'animistic', the *Life-force* or *Vital-force* is the essential force which moves everything. This force exists in everything and, disguised as everchanging matter, it is the dynamic manifestation of an All-Pervading Energy or Spirit. One can, if one wishes view it as a form of pantheism. It can alternatively be viewed, if one is a puritanical materialist, as a form of atheism depending on whether one prefers to be more scientific and substitute the term 'energy' for 'spirit'.

Logical Consistency and Coherence of African Worldview

Because of the language and the culture in which the present debate is being held, and because of the present hegemony of Western culture over world culture, we are forced to use Western science as our frame of reference in examining African science. Because Western science does not deal with the psychic or spiritual element, we must temporarily ignore it in trying to show that African beliefs form a coherent system and concentrate only on physical science.

The fundamental subjects of physical science are space, time, matter and energy; or if we talk in the context where Einstein's theory of relativity is applicable (i.e., for objects which move close to the speed of light) these subjects are reduced from four to two: space-time and matter-energy. We shall look at the African concepts of these same subjects with the object of showing that African concepts of space, time, matter and energy are the very same concepts implied by the theory of relativity. This goes to imply the systematic nature of African thought; unless, of course, one sees these concurrences of African belief with relativity physics as purely coincidental. It should follow that if African beliefs form a coherent system then, since we are all rational beings, this system should be translatable into the scientific language of another culture. We begin by comparing African and relativistic concepts of space and time.

In his book, *Special Theory of Relativity*, David Bohm attempts to describe Einsteinian concepts of space and time by first of all describing the 'common sense' Western notions of them. In his own words they entail supposing space and time to be like '... self existent and flowing substances which are essentially independent of all relationships'.[20]

In African thought space is a matrix of objects. It is not, as commonly thought of in the Western world, the ether or void which envelopes and lies between all objects while existing independently of them. On the contrary, it is constituted of the objects themselves. Says Mbiti: 'As with time, it is the content which defines space'.[21]

African time is a concatenation or chain of events, not

some ethereal stream which flows independent of events and against which events are measured. Time is the succession of events themselves.

As in relativity physics, matter and energy in the African system are one and the same. This energy takes the form of forces which are the very essence of matter. Says Nkrumah in speaking about the African idea of matter: '... matter is not just dead weight, but alive with forces in tension. Indeed for the African everything that exists, exists as a complex of forces in tension'.[22] We are able to see the resemblance between the African idea and that of relativity physics when Bohm describes matter by distinguishing between what he calls 'energies of outward and inward movement':

> On the one hand there is the energy of outward movement which occurs on the large scale, for example, when a body changes position or orientation as a whole. On the other hand, there is the energy of inward movement, for example, the thermal motions of the constituent molecules, which cancel out on the large scale.[23]

We note, to put it all in a nutshell, that the African idea of matter is of matter being a plenum of forces in tension (that is, matter is latent energy). This is precisely the idea modern physicists have. We note that the inward movement of molecules which cancel out on the large scale in Bohm's description are precisely the complex of forces in tension in the African description. This description given by Nkrumah is an echo of what anthropologists such as Tempels and, later on, Jahn have said. Tempels says,

> We can conceive of the transcendental notion of 'being' by separating it from its attribute, 'Force', but the Bantu cannot. 'Force' in his thought is a necessary element in 'being' and the concept of 'force' is inseparable from the definition of 'being'. There is no idea among the Bantu of 'being' divorced from the idea of 'force' ...
> 'We hold a static conception of "being", they a dynamic'.[24]

Though Tempels' manner is extremely patronising his words help us to conclude that since the four fundamental subjects of physical science: space, time, matter and energy are conceived in precisely the same way in African philosophy as they are conceived in relativity physics, it is implied that African beliefs are not just an assortment of quaint and exotic ideas but a logically consistent and coherent system of knowledge.

There is, however, an important and fundamental aspect in which African beliefs differ from modern Western science which relates to the living nature of all matter. In the African universe nothing is dead, not even a stone, which is in stark contrast to the Western idea of matter. What will be known here as the 'Dead Matter Thesis' in Western thought probably began with Isaac Newton and may well have evolved more as a result of political and theological necessity than intellectual necessity, in order to avoid being persecuted for heresy like his forerunner, Galileo, by a church whose theological doctrine pronounced God as a creator external to His creation. Such a doctrine was plainly contradicted by any idea of animate matter and Newton, who had much respect for Egyptian knowledge, was bound to base his science on the notion of the passivity or lifelessness of matter. Says Bernal:

> Toland had absorbed many of Bruno's cosmological Hermetic and Egyptian ideas of animate matter and a world spirit, ideas which lead to pantheism and even atheism. Long before this Newton himself had hesitated, in private, on the question of the activity or passivity of matter, but Newtonianism was not merely scientific. It had a consequent political and theological doctrine which depended on the passivity of matter, with motion coming only from the outside. Otherwise, theologically, the universe would need no creator ...[25]

In regard to the Western 'Dead Matter Thesis', Nkrumah notes:

> Now if one wishes to maintain the philosophical inertness of matter, one must ascribe the phenomenal self motion of

bodies to some non-material principle, usually a soul or a spirit. This soul or spirit may of course be said to inhere in matter or to be external to it.[26]

One cannot argue matter to be totally inert or dead if the spirit which moves it inheres within it; for the soul or spirit would then be an essential aspect of the matter itself. The notion of dead or inert matter definitely requires that one ascribes the motion of matter to some non-material principle which is external to matter. Thus Newton's rejection of the activity of matter fell in line with his religious beliefs as well as his concern not to offend religious authority. Westerners, consequently, inherited the notion of a Supreme Being very much estranged from and extraneous to nature. The supposition of the activity of matter leads, on the contrary, to a system where the Supreme Being is identified with nature.

To most Western educated or conditioned minds the activity or living nature of matter may seem a strange notion. However, it is one which is consistent with our everyday observations of things. We start from the African premise that everything has its own level of consciousness or vital force and thus its own level of response to external action from other objects. There is a hierarchy of forces descending from human beings through to the animals, the plants, and finally reaching stones and rocks at the lower end.[27] But nothing is dead. In the Western mode of thought many of the responses we observe in lesser objects are interpreted as being *passive*, but seen in another light they could just as well be interpreted as *active* responses. For example, if a person drops a glass bottle on a pavement it will smash. Because we are conditioned by the Western mode of thought to think of the bottle as being 'dead', we interpret the smashing of the bottle into pieces as consistent with its passivity. But could this not also be seen as the bottle's own level of *active* response to the action of being dropped onto a pavement? If a man throws a stone at a second man, the instinctive response of the second man would be to duck. We accept this to be the response of a living being. Is this response so different from that of the bottle which scatters into pieces on being dropped onto hard ground? Similarly, if I kick a person hard enough that person will shout. If I kick the door of a car hard enough it will dent. The car door has its own level of *active* response to my action, which is to dent. Whilst Western science and philosophy strives to discover what constitutes consciousness, African philosophy and the philosophy of other peoples of colour holds merely that consciousness is an intrinsic aspect of matter. What remains to be discovered, therefore, is not what constitutes consciousness but rather what constitutes the various levels of consciousness.

AFRICAN ART

As has already been noted, art in Africa does not exist for art's sake. Segy's observation in regard to African sculpture could just as well apply to African art as a whole:

'African carvings, I must first emphasize most strongly, were not considered "works of art" in our sense of the term. They were "useful objects"; they were implements used, for the most part, in religious and magical ceremonies which often formed the basis for their social organizations. African carvings had a definite role in the life of the African; without them, in many cases, he could not have functioned in his society; perhaps he could not have survived'.[28]

Thus African art is primarily functional and for this reason the approach taken here to the discussion of African art is to focus on its various uses in African society which include it being a form of documentation for historical information as well as religious and philosophical ideas in symbolic form, being a means to concretise the invisible spirit world or to bring the sub-conscious into the conscious, and finally for entertainment and aesthetic pleasure.

African Art as a Means of Documentation

African art is a means of documentation, not only of historical events but also of a people's worldview. This is especially so in regard to mythology which is often the well spring of inspiration for African art.[29]

The author, Roy Sieber notes that art generally can function as a means of communication. In art it is the mode or form of communication which is important. 'Art must be persuasive in terms of what we normally call the aesthetic, but persuasive about something else – the idea or symbol. The aesthetic is a tool by which the artist persuades us that an idea or concept is meaningful. It is a way of saying something that cannot be said as effectively in any other manner'.[30]

It does happen that certain levels of meaning which exist in African art are accessible only to a few individuals, for example, the initiates of secret societies. Religious ideas have created many of the symbols present in the art and some of these ideas are known only by initiates.[31] The reason for guarding these ideas are generally not malevolent. Knowledge is power and can be a danger to the community if this falls into the hands of one who is morally unprepared. Thus it is restricted to initiates who have undergone rigorous moral training. Professor Wingert appears to equate the secret societies of Africa with the secret societies of the west when he attributes their secretive nature to a need for power and control over the community. He says:

'The beings represented by the Ibibio and the Sulka masks have, as secret society property, two sets of meanings: for the nonmembers, the forms express the danger and menace of the unworldly, weird, supernatural spirits depicted by the objects and their actions; for the members they mean disguises with which the activities of the group are accomplished'.[32]

Wingert seems to reduce the religio-social significance of the masks to that of a mere disguise used to terrorise the community and hide the identity of the secret society so they could continue terrorising and exercising power and influence over the community. If we are to interpret secret societies in Africa as Wingert does they are groups who see their own religious beliefs as a fraud to be used on the people to achieve their own ends. The enlightened nature of the secret society in Wingert's interpretation would seem to relate to an awareness of the fraudulent nature of their religious beliefs rather than a more profound understanding of them.

African Art as a Means of Concretising the Invisible Spirit World

The African mask deserves special attention as it is the chief implement of the ritual. Through the masks unseen spirits were cast into the visible world and the masks were seen as their abode. Masks were thus symbolic of the spirits, they were not identified with the spirits (that is, African people do not believe the sculptures themselves to be the spirits). In looking at the mask it is vital to look at the art dynamically in the context of its function in ritual as opposed to looking at it as a static work of art as is unfortunately the case for some of the stolen African masks that grace western museums. The ritual celebrates the oneness of human beings with nature and forms a bridge between the visible and invisible worlds through the invocation of unseen spirits. The ritual also served as a means of restoring social cohesion and the standard of morality and order handed down by ancestors hence maintaining the balance or equilibrium in the society.[33] This might involve the call for guidance in one of the passing rites (i.e., birth, initiation, marriage, death) or the call for rain or protection from disease.[34] The mask, which harbours the spirit-force is used to call the spirits of the gods and ancestors for guidance and protection. This could also be achieved through carved wooden figures of the ancestors which contained the spirit of the ancestor and were the 'visible and tangible means by which the spiritual force or power of the ancestor was contacted'.[35]

In the ritual we come across the setting in which the arts come together. Music, sculpture, dance drama and poetry are all there at once. The masked dancer acts out the role of the spirit he represents. In order to emphasize the non-human nature of the spirit he often wore a large brightly coloured attire mainly made of raffia and leaves and with amulets attached. The dancer is required to be impersonal in the ritual in the sense that in the course of the ritual his own personality becomes one and the same with that of the spirit. Says Segy: 'This was possible because by obliterating his self awareness, the dancer was able to enter into the level on which the spirit was believed to exist and to communicate with it in the here

Fig. 11 Ivory Mask, Benin Kingdom, Nigeria used as a pectoral by the Oba (King).

and now'.[36] As Segy goes on to note, the audience was part of this 'happening' with each individual being fused into a collective consciousness that is in a heightened state. In a 'prescribed, institutionalised' manner a bridge is crossed between the worlds of the sensible and the supersensible achieving the intimate union with nature, social cohesion and equilibrium that are the goals of the ritual.

It is interesting to note in passing that other peoples of colour use the mask similarly, uniting the cultures of Africa, Oceania and Native America.[37] The identification of the masked dancer with the represented spirit also occurs in the rituals of the Iroquois native Americans, for Wingert says, 'Each carved mask represented the actual presence of a supernatural being, and the wearer, for the duration of the ceremony, lost his own identity'.[38]

'Masks are the symbols of spiritual forces that validate the acts and precepts of the elders'.[39] The mask is thus a symbol of authority and is therefore used in cases where a dispute may occur in the community to restore equilibrium and social cohesion. 'It represents the spirit force which, transcending the more usual symbols, represents the ultimate force – the god spirit – that gives final approval or disapproval of the decisions used by the elders'.[40] In concluding this description of the role of the mask in African society borrowed from Sieber, we might make the interesting comparison between the wig and gown of the Western judge in which all the power and authority of the law is symbolically invested and the symbol of authority provided by the mask.

The spirits evoked through the use of the masks and figures are ancestral. Sieber notes that ancestor figures are a major aspect of African art. The most representational figures in African art, which is largely an abstract or conceptual art, are those of past kings and queens (for instance, the Ife and Bushongo portraits).

African art is rarely representational. One might connect these special instances of representational work to the African concept or belief in personal immortality in which the deceased lives on through the remembrance of the name or any other aspect of the person. In this case, personal immortality is enhanced by the representational sculpture by sustaining in the minds of future generations, the facial likeness of the ancestor.[41] Generally, the idea was not to duplicate or copy observed

Fig. 12 Brass Head of a ruler. Ife, Nigeria. (Museum of Mankind, London.) This representational style may be connected with the religious concept of personal immortality whereby the subject is immortalised through the remembrance of the facial likeness.

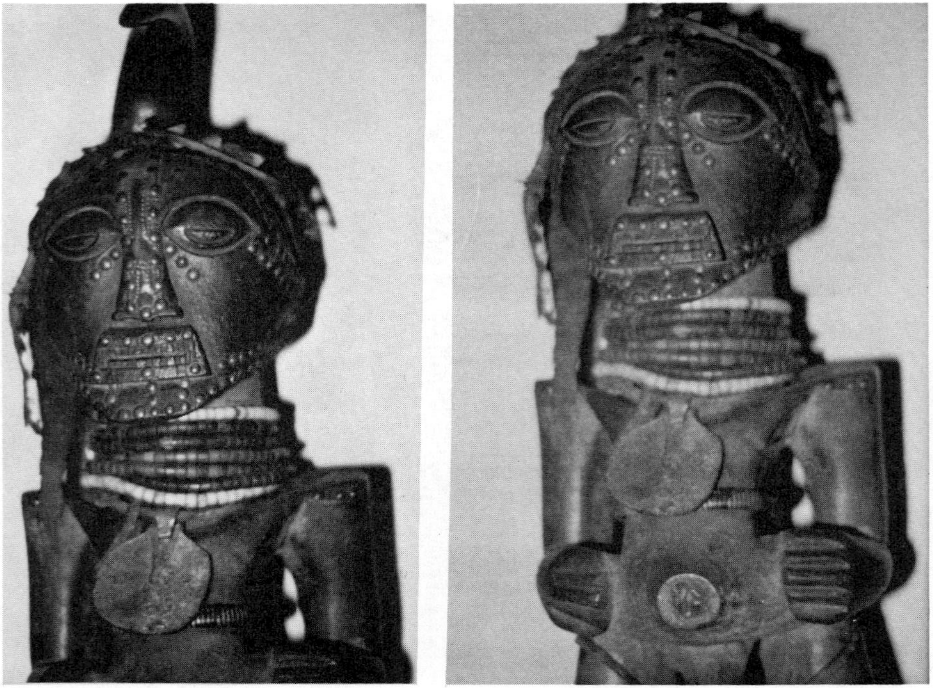

Figs. 13a/13b Wood and metal Basongye Sculpture, Zaire. (Museum of Mankind, London.)

reality and the abstraction of the human facial features from observed reality served to express the spiritual, which is beyond the visible world.[42]

We note that African masks can at times appear terrific. This form of facial expression was related to the warding off of evil spirits which brought drought, disease, pestilence and other mishaps.[43] Wingert interprets the terrific expression of some African masks quite differently assuming that they were used by secret societies to conjure evil spirits that aided them in terrorising and subjugating the community to their control and rule of law.[44]

One who is familiar with African art cannot help but notice the fact that it is largely abstract. This is significant; for even African scholars of religion, philosophy and anthropology have been bought by what can only be described as the racist Western anthropological view that the thought forms of African and other peoples of colour are more concrete than abstract, implying a severely limited capacity for abstract thought. There is plainly no need nowadays to take such a statement seriously, but the obvious abstract or conceptual nature of African and 'Third World' art creates a glaring contradiction to this view. European art on the other hand has traditionally been naturalistic or representational in which the goal of the artist was merely the reproduction of what he saw. With the advent of photography the role of the naturalistic artist must have been questioned.

Segy states that abstract art in general 'is not an intellectual exercise but is based upon man's natural need to express his inner world in appropriate abstract forms'.[45] In Africa art is primarily about bringing man's and woman's inner world into the outside world. This is the basic philosophy of surrealism. This and other seminal art movements in the Western world owe their existence to African art.

In regard to this we note that African art forms are often geometric. It was this aspect that lead to European Cubism, the most important of the modern art movements. In talking of the geometric form in African art the American mathematician Claudia Zaslavsky observes:

Fig. 14 Wooden Bamana figure of a Woman, Mali, W. Africa. (Museum of Mankind, London.)
Pre-cubistic style figure showing that the use of geometric shapes was not only characteristic of sculpture from Central Africa, but of African sculpture on the whole.

The tendency to distort natural forms for the purpose of stressing certain characteristics, and the wide application of symbol motifs in decoration lead to an emphasis on the geometric aspect in African art. European Cubism of the early twentieth century took its inspiration from the sculpture of Africa. As just one example, the concave faces of Picasso's 'Les Demoiselles d'Avignon' resemble the masks of the Kwele, Kota and other peoples of the Congo.[46]

It is sometimes asked which is the first of the arts in Africa. To answer this we might refer to the myths of creation. Prevalent on the continent is the idea of God as the potter who made the first human being out of clay. Thus the art of sculpture was realised. But even before this the world was brought into being through the utterance of the Word. This utterance was also a rhythmic vibration. Thus it would appear that music as a fundamental rhythmic form and poetry as the rhythmic utterance of the Word came into being. The basis of music in Africa is the rhythm of the drums which speak the tones of most African languages, since African languages are musical or tonal. If one listens to the drum music of a particular area and then listens to the speech of the people of that area one will almost always, if not always, notice a similarity between the way in which the drum tones rise and fall and the speech tones rise and fall. Jahn observes that African drum language is not a code which has to be translated into the local language by following some set of rules; it is a direct means of communication in the local language.[47] The following observation made by Nketia serves to explain how this is done, by reference to the manner in which meaning changes with variation in the speech tone:

> Whatever the scale attention is paid as far as possible to the intonation of the text. This is because distortion of the intonation of phrases or the tones of words might create problems for the listener, for many African languages are 'tone languages', that is languages in which tone ... serves to distinguish words in much the same way as do vowels or consonants.[48]

In other words, a word may have several different meanings depending on where the emphasis is placed in pronunciation. To take a simple example from the author's native language, Igbo, the word spelt as 'oke' can have two meanings depending on where the emphasis is placed. The emphasis is denoted with a stroke above the appropriate letter:

òke – rat
òkè – a share or a portion

To take a parallel example in musical terms, a beat given as 4/4 time (i.e., four beats to the bar) can be played in many different ways depending on where the accent is placed. It could, for instance, be played as three soft beats followed by a hard beat or soft-hard-soft-hard or hard-soft-soft-soft, etc. It is because of this phenomenon that Western musical notation is inadequate for documenting the complex rhythms of African music, especially where there are cross rhythms, i.e., many rhythmic variations happening simultaneously.

In African music, variations of tone mimic the variation of human speech; but variation of tone alone is not enough to create the 'speech music' which is characteristic of African musical style. According to Ortiz Walton [49], quoting Ekundayo Phillips in his support, speech music is created and the sense of syncopation heightened through the variation of rhythm as well as tone. Placing emphasis on parts of the music through playing just slightly 'off-beat' or 'displacing' the accent is what is known as *syncopation*, and is characteristic of most African music including jazz. Above, the terms 'off-beat' and 'displaced' are, however, culturally relative and Eurocentric: 'off-beat' and 'displaced' to the European ear may not be so to the African ear where these subtle variations merely reflect the structure of African languages. It is because of this phenomenon that African music defies adequate documentation using Western musical notation, especially where there are complex rhythms known as *cross-rhythms*; that is many rhythmic variations happening simultaneously, yet interweaving harmoniously into an integrated whole.

Part II

THE SELF AND THE EXTERNAL WORLD

INTRODUCTION

In Dogon cosmology the human being is the micro-cosmic replica of the external universe[1] and in ancient Egyptian cosmology the development of human consciousness is symbolised by the myth of the creation of the universe. In the beginning there is chaos which becomes ordered according to the plan of the divine intelligence, Thoth. In the development of human consciousness there is likewise an initial chaos since the infant first perceives only of a world of confusion from which he does not perceive himself as distinct.[2] However, after he has developed a concept of a self and becomes conscious of himself as being distinct from what he experiences, he begins to develop all the Ideas and concepts which will enable his coherent perception of reality (e.g., space, time, substance, permanence, etc.). Another comparison rests in the cosmological idea of the universe as originating from a single source: in the same way, consciousness (that is, true consciousness which involves the ability to reflect upon one's thoughts, sensations and emotions) has the concept of the self, a unity, as its source.

Thus from a duality of Being and Becoming we move to the duality (though this is not a duality of opposites) of the human being and the external world in which the pair of Being and Becoming are incorporated; for the universe and the human being are both spiritual and material. Human consciousness is a reflection of the universe, and each individual is like one among myriad mirror spheres each reflecting the world from their own viewpoint in space and time.

Space and time are the dimensions of the universe and also appear to be dimensions of consciousness. One should not be surprised, therefore, to find them intimately related to its eventual orientation. The fact that there are cultural variations in the conceptions of space and time means there also exist differences (though not vast ones) in what various cultures regard as 'common sense'. 'Common sense' is relative. We shall see that this is true, especially in regard to variations between traditional African and traditional Western conceptions of time.

1.
THE DEVELOPMENT OF HUMAN CONSCIOUSNESS

DEVELOPMENT OF INTELLIGENCE IN THE CHILD

Self consciousness consists in the possession of a concept of the self through awareness of the external world. It can be shown by present psychological evidence from the studies of the development of intelligence in young children that external objects cannot be perceived discriminately until the child has first of all developed a concept of the self. Among these undiscriminated objects is himself. Bohm writes on the development of perception in young children: 'The very young infant does not behave as if he had the adult's concept of a world separate from himself. Piaget[1] gives good evidence suggesting that the infant begins by experiencing an almost undifferentiated totality. That is to say, he has not yet learned to distinguish between what arises inside and outside of him, nor to distinguish between the various aspects of the "outer" and "inner" worlds. Instead there is experienced only one world, in a state of continual flux of sensations, perceptions, feelings, etc. ... with nothing recognisable as permanent in it'.[2] Referring to the stage at which the concept of self has emerged he says '... the child begins to see clearly the distinction between himself and the rest of the world .... In his new mental "map" of the world he can maintain a permanent distinction between himself and other objects. Everything on this map falls into two categories – what is "inside his skin" and what is not. He learns to associate various feelings, pleasures, pains, desires, etc., with what is "inside his skin", and thus he forms the concept of a "self", distinct from the rest of the world ...'.[3]

It seems that in forming a concept of the self the child has formed a point of reference from which he views the world. He is then able to distinguish himself from the object he experiences; he is then able to distinguish one object as being different from another; he is then also able to perceive motion which requires that he is able to recognise an object as being the same object at different instances in its motion.

At this point we must be clear on which self it is we are talking of. Is this concept of self a reference to the physical self, made up of the body and the personality we abstract from the speech, movement and mannerisms of the person; or is it an immaterial or spiritual self? As conscious beings we possess the power to reflect upon our actions sensations and emotions and even thoughts. In all of these phenomena we perceive change, difference, motion. In fact, we cannot deny that our physical and mental selves form a part of the ever-changing world. But, we note that, by the doctrine of opposites, in order to know change, motion, and difference we must also know constancy, stillness and identity. This sense of constancy, stillness and identity is plainly not to be found in the body's or the mind's ever fluctuating sensations, emotions and thoughts. It must involve the notion of a self beyond the physical.

Everyone of us of necessity possesses the concept of an immaterial self beyond the physical; for this is a precondition before coherent experience of the world can be possible. It is proposed that this conception of an immaterial self is of a unity or oneness which maintains its identity through time and lies 'somewhere' deep within us. It is the very Idea of Permanent Self we discussed towards the end of Part One.

We have now broken down the rather ethereal concept of a soul or immaterial self into the two concepts of unity (oneness) and identity (sameness). These are basically the concepts which, so it is supposed, constitute the notion of a soul. They could not have developed from experience for possession of them is the very condition under which coherent experience is possible. These concepts are known by intuition; how else could they have been acquired?

FUNDAMENTAL CONCEPTS OF THE SELF

Awareness of a unity and identity at the centre of one's being which is somehow apart from one's physical nature is self consciousness; which is inseparably related to awareness of one's physical self as a complex of actions, sensations, emotions and thoughts. Unity and identity are therefore seen as self consciousness' dual aspects and need to be defined:

Unity. A quality (not a property)[4] which may be attributed to any object given to us in experience; that is, everything in experience has the quality of being 'one', e.g., a person is 'one' person, a tree is 'one' tree, etc.

Identity. The concept of an object in experience firstly, being identical with itself (an analytical truth) and secondly, remaining the same object through time, i.e., retaining its identity through time.

For the origin of these concepts we need to look beyond sense experience. Psychologists have known for some time that we cannot properly perceive objects without concepts or form concepts without percepts. In other words, what we experience through our senses is determined by what we know, and what we know is determined by what we have experienced. This draws us into a vicious circle: for how then could the perceptual process in the new-born infant begin?

The argument put forward here is that the infant's first perception of the world is simultaneous with his first conception of it. In other words, the first moment of human consciousness would appear to be a miracle. However, in the African worldview this is more a transition than a miracle since every object in the world possesses some level of consciousness. There is merely the question of the moment at which there is a transition into the realm of *human* consciousness. Self consciousness in the African worldview is not an isolated phenomenon, in the sense that self awareness necessarily involves the awareness of the external world. The individual's existence is interconnected with that of his or her community and environment, the people and the things among which he or she exists. It is, as John Mbiti says, a case of 'I am because we are, and since we are therefore I am.'[5] The individual's existence is seen as corporate with that of his or her community and environment. This, as we shall see further on, has important consequences for African ethics and the notion of moral responsibility. In a nutshell, the respect for the well being of our fellow women and men as well as for all other living things as reflected in a conservationist attitude towards animals, plants and the soil is tied to our own individual survival.

It makes sense to suppose first perception and first conception as being simultaneous. Self awareness (conception of a self) would thus be simultaneous with awareness of the external world (perception of other people and things). It would seem that one involves the other and is inseparable from the other. To have the sensation of touching is at the same time to be aware of being touched. There is a two-way dialectical relationship. The physical contact between mother and infant is therefore a first crucial state in the child's formation of a concept of the self. We note that when the baby begins to crawl there is the need to explore by touching things.

Thus self consciousness must involve a consciousness of the external world. The truth, manifested in the process of early human development, is indeed the key to African people's way of life which Segy describes as 'The dissolution of the individual into the collective consciousness'.[6]

However, despite the simultaneity of first perception and first conception it is still supposed that prior to experience we possess two fundamental concepts that are fundamental aspects of self consciousness which are somehow inbuilt in us. These are the concepts of Unity and Identity.

We must note that experience is particular to each individual. The experience of each individual is unique to that individual alone. The first lines of a poem written by a friend of mine beautifully illustrate the manner in which nature harmoniously synthesizes individuality and universality: 'I am unique. Just like everybody is'.

Despite our individual uniqueness as brought about by the diversity of our experiences there is a common ground of consciousness that we all share. Though we may disagree on questions of art and morality we cannot disagree on such irrevocable truths as '1 = 1' or 'a cat is a cat'. Such truths are called *analytic* truths and all logic and mathematics are composed of such statements, although they can become much more complex. We notice also that the entire mathematical universe is available to each one of us without exception. The only barriers are limitations on the skill with which we use the available tools (i.e., how skilfully we are able to apply the rules and principles). As a simple example of this we note that we can all agree on the numbers which form the set of whole numbers 1, 2, 3, 4, 5, 6, 7, ... etc., or on the set of whole numbers which are divisible by 2: 2, 4, 6, 8, 10, ... etc., or the set of whole numbers which are divisible by 13: 13, 26, 39, 52, ... etc. The only thing which prevents some of us agreeing is the level of skill with which we are able to apply the rules, in this case it is the level of skill with which we are able to add and to divide. We agree on such things without consulting the outside world. These mathematical universes are somehow *within* us.

Some have thought of this common ground of consciousness, which is the 'landscape' of mathematics and logic, as a manifestation of the Divine Mind which is all-pervading. It reminds us of the ancient African god, *Thoth*, the Divine Intelligence or Universal Mind, the inventor of the arts and sciences and scribe of the moral law of whom the goddess *Maat* is the female counterpart.[7]

This mystical oneness which unites all despite life's diversity is associated with the concepts of Unity and Identity, the fundamental aspects of self consciousness. Two general arguments are followed to show that these concepts are given to our intuition (i.e., that they are inbuilt and not derived from experience). The first is derived from Kant. We begin with the concept of unity. The general argument for its intuitive origin rests in the Kantian notion of the 'unity of self consciousness'.[8] The unity of self consciousness is shown by the fact that we perceive all objects as unities. It is impossible to perceive anything otherwise. A group of objects may be perceived as one (i.e., *one* group of objects); in this case the group itself becomes the object. We are only able to focus attention on a single object or detail at a time; we can only think a single thought at a time. All that I perceive is apprehended with the consciousness that these percepts belong to me and to me alone; they are seen from my unique point of view. There is only one of me in the world and nobody else sees the world through my own consciousness, which must therefore be essentially *one*. This is undeniably individualistic, but this individual consciousness is at the same time inseparable from the external world, for awareness of the external world is a necessity for the existence of individual consciousness. Consciousness can only exist as a consciousness of *something* and the external world is that which constitutes consciousness.

It could never be upheld that the concept of unity comes from sense experience. Frege, with the support of Baumann, argues convincingly that number is not a property of external things;[9] for although every object can be attributed with oneness there is never anything in the object which conveys this oneness. For example, a tree is *one* tree but there is nothing visible about the tree which conveys oneness. An object may be attributed with being 'blue' or being 'round'; these are visible properties, unlike the concept of number. It is the view of this author that whereas the idea of multiplicity (the concept of *many*) comes from sense experience, the concept of unity is intuitive. As we have noted, life is a concert of opposites. There can be no multiplicity without unity, because a multiplicity is made up of unities.

The derivation of the concept of identity from intuition is perhaps far more evident. It is not through experience that we infer that an object is identical with itself just as experience doesn't tell us that $1 = 1$. Nothing in the object could possibly convey this apparently trivial morsel of knowledge. To say that a thing is identical with itself is equivalent with saying $1 = 1$. All arithmetic and most of mathematics is constituted of such truths, though they vary in complexity. The concept of identity represents the most fundamental form of all such statements; hence, trivial though it may seem, this concept is fundamental to our very ability to reason – it is the foundation of logical thought, and therefore the source of arithmetic and mathematical thought.

At the same time that the concept of the self emerges, the concepts of space and time are also acquired.[10] Their source is to be traced to the notions of the unity and identity of the self. Whereas unity is a *formal* concept and therefore progenitor of the idea of space, the concept of enduring identity enables the perception of change and motion and is therefore the origin of the idea of time.

2.
THE COSMOLOGY

Fig. 15 The Star Sirius and its Dwarf Companion (lower right) – Original germ of life.

Ancient Dogon mythology surrounds Sirius and its tiny companion Sirius B. The Dogon say that Sirius B (the tiny seed '*Kizi Uzi*') is the most important star in the sky, is heavier than all the material on earth and orbits Sirius every 50 years. It is that to which they trace the origin of the universe; it is the original seed of life. The Dogon claim that Sirius has another companion which is light with almost circular orbit. Sirius B is invisible to the naked eye and was only discovered by western scientists in 1862. The Dogon Sirius tradition is at least 700 years old. It is something else they have in common with the ancient Egyptians. Western scientists found that Sirius B is made of dense matter and orbits Sirius every 50 years – just as the Dogon have believed for the past 700 years! (See H.H. Adams, *Blacks in Science*, p.29.)

ANCIENT EGYPTIAN, DOGON AND BAMBARA ACCOUNTS OF THE CREATION

Despite the migration and spread of African people throughout the continental land mass from the origins of civilization along the Nile Valley, the original cosmological theme of African religion remains basically intact. Some African peoples today have diverged more than others away from the original cosmology. Still there remains an underlying thread of consistency to all. Fundamentally, most accounts mention or have implicit within them a primeval void or water; the preconception by a divine mind or predetermination of the plan of the world which is about to be created and finally the conception of this plan in the form of the spoken divine word. These are the basic principles which, one might note, are exactly analogous to the mundane. The primeval void or water may be thought of as symbolic of a mother's womb; the preconception in the divine mind may be thought of as symbolic of the fertilized egg which possess all the genetic traits of the unborn child; the emission of the divine word from the mouth of the creator is symbolic of the conception of the child or the chick bursting forth from its shell. We see from this and other examples the power of analogy in helping us to understand the significance of mythology in African religion.

In presenting actual examples we again strive to represent both the traditional and the ancient. The cosmology of the Dogon of Mali and the Bambara of Guinea, on the traditional side, are here described along side further versions of the ancient Egyptian cosmology.

In the Dogon creation myth as described by Griaule and Dieterlen[1] the original germ of life is symbolised by the smallest created seed, Digitaria Exilis, which the Dogon know as *kize uzi* ('little thing'). This seed had an internal vibration which caused it to burst out from its casing and emerge to reach the uttermost confines of the universe. At the same time the unfolding matter moved in a spiral or heliacal path, the first revolution of which had seven segments, each of which represents a different level of vibration. These were the first seven vibrations of matter.² Two fundamental principles are expressed by the myth. Firstly, the heliacal movement is often diagrammatically represented by the Dogon as a zig-zag line which represents the alternation between opposites – left and right, up and down, male and female. The support of one opposite by another leads to an equilibrium in nature which is maintained internally by each individual being. This principle of twin-ness or duality gives rise to the proliferation of all life. Secondly, the perpetual movement of matter along this heliacal path expresses the infinite extension of the universe.

Fig 16 The late Dogon sage, Ogotomelli, appointed by the elders to reveal esoteric knowledge to the late anthropologist, Marcel Griaule.

These movements take place inside an ovoid form – 'the egg of the world'. Within the seed or 'egg' is the original germ of life in which all things that are yet to come into being exist, already differentiated in embryo. On the seventh vibration of the first vibrations of matter, the segment formed by the unfolding matter breaks its enveloping casing. Having burst out of its casing the creative process follows its predetermined path.

In Davidson's description of the Bambara account of the

creation, creation arose from the void, *fu*, by the action of *gla*, 'the creating but uncreated principle of fundamental movement of the cosmos and all that therein is, a principle of continuous creation. Full of its emptiness and its emptiness full of itself, *gla*, by uttering a voice from the void, ... created its double *dya*, thus endowing Life with a dialectical force. Out of *gla:dya* there came *zo* the symbol of human consciousness, and *yo*, the symbol of purposive thought. From these the universe was ordered and took shape'.[3]

Before moving on to relate the ancient Egyptian account we might say something about the dialectical twins *gla/dya* and *zo/yo* which might appear unclear in the above account. I understood them like this: *gla/dya* is a *passive* duo. They are principles (or the thoughts of the divine intelligence?). *Gla* is like the concept of nothing existing, and this, by the doctrine of opposites, inevitably leads to *dya*, the concept of *something* existing; for the two are complementary (e.g., darkness presupposes the existence of light). It is by means of these two concepts together as *gla/dya* that the momentum of creation is initiated. *Zo/yo* is the *active* duo. Here we are not just concerned with passive principles, but the divine intelligence which puts them into practice. *Zo/yo* may be conceived as parallel to *gla/dya*. Whereas *zo* is pure consciousness, *yo* is consciousness of an object; that is, purposive thought. Here the existence of *zo* necessitates the existence of *yo*, in the same way that *gla* necessitates *dya*: what is consciousness if it is not a consciousness of something?

Wallis Budge gives the following description of the Egyptian account originating from Brugsch: 'According to the writings of the Egyptians, there was a time when neither heaven nor earth existed, and when nothing had being except the boundless primeval water, which was, however, shrouded with thick darkness. In this condition the primeval water remained for a considerable time, notwithstanding that it contained within it the germs of the things which afterwards came into existence in this world, and the world itself. At length the spirit of the primeval water felt the desire for creative activity, and having uttered the word, the world sprang straightway into being in the form which had already been depicted in the mind of the spirit before he spake the word which resulted in its creation'.[4]

This description is supported by the following account from the *Book of Knowing the Creations of Ra* (papyrus No. 10188, British Museum): 'I am he who evolved himself under the form of the god Khepera. I, the evolver of the evolutions evolved myself, the evolver of all evolutions, after many evolutions and developments *which came forth from my mouth*. No heaven existed and no earth, and no terrestrial animals or reptiles had come into being. I formed them out of the inert mass of watery matter, I found no place whereon to stand .... I was alone, and the gods Shu and Tefnut had not gone forth from me; there existed none other who worked with me. I laid the foundations of all things by my will, and all things evolved themselves therefrom. ... I sent forth Shu and Tefnut out from myself; thus from being one god I became three, and Shu and Tefnut gave birth to Nut and Seb ...'.[5]

Finally, this last version of the Egyptian creation account originating from Amelineau and given in Diop's *African Origin of Civilization* is quoted for its striking similarity to the Bambara account: '... at the beginning there was chaotic, uncreated matter, the primitive Nun (cf. Nen = nothingness, in Wolof[6]). This primitive matter contained, in the form of principles, all possible beings. It also contained the god of potential development, Khepru (Khepera). As soon as the primitive nothingness created Ra, the demi-urge, its role ended'.[7]

All ancient Egyptian accounts begin with the existence of a primeval void or primeval water. It seems that the boundless primeval water is representative of a void in which nothing exists. This void, because it is nothingness, had within itself the potential (or room if you wish) to create everything which could possibly exist. This potential for creation is represented by Khepru (or *gla/dya* in the Bambara account). The demi-urge, Ra (or *zo/yo* in the Bambara account), can be thought of as a longing by the emptiness to fill itself. From this we see that the ancient Egyptians thought of the world as being, fundamentally, a duality of void and matter, a conception of the world attributed to the Atomists, Leucippus (whose existence is doubted[8]) and Democritus of 450 B.C.

The existence of a void is something that has traditionally been difficult for the down-to-earth person to accept; since the notion is supremely abstract. For this reason, it is believed, the Egyptians often conceived of it as a boundless watery abyss. One might wish to note, however, that Carruthers, for one, sees them as being distinct. He says: 'The self created creator did not, however, accidently emerge from a void but from Nnw (the primeval water ...)'.[9] The void is in essence not subject to experience or conception and cannot therefore be either demonstrated or refuted to exist. Most of the remaining chapter is concerned with showing that this notion of emptiness is present in us, only it is hidden by and confused within modern 'common sense' notions of time and, most evidently, space.

CONCEPTS OF SPACE AND TIME

Western traditional notions of space and time appear to be absolutist in that they suppose space and time to have existences independent of the world they are thought to contain. However, in the African view they are not to be distinguished from the material world; that is space and time, on the one hand, and objects and events, on the other, are not essentially different. In regard to time being intrinsically related to events in the African mentality, Mbiti notes that instead of numerical calendars representative of the Western linear concept of time Africans possess 'phenomenon calendars' which are dictated by events.[10] For instance, in Africa when older people without formal education are asked their age they do not give a date, but relate their age to a significant event which took place about the same time; to narrow this down reference would be made to the fact that it was the time of the rains or of the drought in recalling the time of the year. In regard to space Mbiti notes as with time that it is the content of space (i.e., objects) which define it. Also space and time are so closely linked that often the same word is used for both.[11] Not so long ago these notions of space and time might have been thought primitive; but they are today seen to be consistent with modern science.

A curious difference exists between traditional African and traditional Western ideas of time which Mbiti has studied: '...

time is simply a composition of events which have occurred, those which are taking place now and those which are immediately to occur. What has not taken place or what has no likelihood of an immediate occurrence falls in the category of "no – time". What is certain to occur or what falls within the rhythm of natural phenomena, is in the category of inevitable or potential time'.[12]

Mbiti goes on to say that the consequence of this is a concept of time with a long past, a present and virtually no future in contrast to the Western concept in which there is an indefinite past, a present and an infinite future. In Swahili the remote past is known as the *Zamani*; whilst the dimension spanning the immediate past, the present and the immediate future is known as the *Sasa*. Thus instead of the Western conception of history moving ahead into an unknown perhaps ominous future, life is conceived as an unfolding revelation in which history flows backwards into the past making way for new revelation in the present. This conception of time has been negatively misconceived by Europeans who wish to explain the African condition in terms of an inferiority of the African. It has been said, for instance, that the virtual absence of a future in African thought explains our inability to make long term plans and hence to govern ourselves. In fact, a host of European imposed forces and contradictions, which we shall touch on briefly further on, are apparent in explaining the failure of government in modern Africa. It is not our manner of thinking which has led to this failure, but rather, the contradictions which arise from the imposition of foreign systems, beliefs, values, etc. On the contrary, our philosophy of time is a positive asset; for it is an attitude conducive to peace of mind and stability, as opposed to the anxiety, instability and fear of being flung into an uncertain future which is implied by the Western conception. The absence of future in African time does not imply stagnation, for it is not a total absence. What future there is, is what Mbiti calls 'potential time' and this consists in events that are likely to occur and whose signs are visible in the present. Often these events can be affected by action in the present. The future is thus not to be seen as so much of a threat, since by living consciously and diligently in the moment and taking it in one's stride the immediate future, which falls within the inevitable rhythm of time, cannot take one by surprise. *Life is meant to be lived at nature's pace; it should not be a race to out run time itself*.

Space and time are seen here as two fundamental aspects of our experience of the world. They represent, it seems, two fundamental aspects of matter: physical extension (i.e., form) and physical transition (i.e., change and motion). In other words, space and time are not to be distinguished from objects and events. Perhaps the reader needs to be convinced of this. To demonstrate that this is the case we examine a couple of examples designed to prove the case both for space and for time. Beforehand we need to look at the Western traditional notions of time and space to compare them and also to see how the notion of emptiness (void) is confused with them. This is taken to imply that the notion of a void, which cannot be refuted or proven to exist by reason, is present in the human intuition. What are shortly described as Western traditional concepts are also mathematical. However, actual space and actual time are different from the mathematical concepts. Mathematical concepts of space and time facilitate the application of science to nature and are in this sense legitimate. Nevertheless, the philosopher or philosophical scientist should always remain aware that they cannot represent the true state of nature.

Western Traditional (and Mathematical) Notion of Space: Is of a void or emptiness which envelopes all objects and exists independently of them. In a consideration of two separated objects, space is held to be the void which lies between and around them. Hence in the Western traditional notion of space it has no reference to objects.

Western Traditional (and Mathematical) Notion of Time: Is of time as flowing without dependence on the events which happen. In the consideration of two events which happen in succession, the temporal gulf between them is a duration of time held to exist in its own right; even if these two events were the only ever to happen, this void would still be considered to possess some definite 'duration'. Such a notion of time has no reference to events.

In showing, on the contrary that space and time cannot exist independent of events, we first of all take the most evident case of space and thereafter time.

A. The Case for Space. In order to show that space cannot exist without objects we try to imagine a solitary object in a void, a sphere, uniform in every physical sense: (1) *The sphere would have no position (i.e., no place)*: Since every 'part' of a void is uniform one could never distinguish one 'part' from another, and there could, therefore, be no place (space). (2) *The sphere would have no size.* Since no external standard of measurement (i.e., no other object) would exist, the sphere could not have size.[13] The concept of size could not have meaning without the possibility of measurement, and this in turn requires the existence of at least another object so that either object could possess size relative to the other. A solitary object in a void could not meaningfully be called 'big' or 'small'.

Due to the demonstrated fact that the sphere neither has size nor position, it cannot be said to occupy a space, and this is the direct result of there being no other objects to provide external standards of reference.

B. The Case for Time. Similarly, to show that time cannot exist without events we consider a solitary event in a void in which nothing else ever existed (or will ever exist). We suppose this event is the appearance and disappearance of the uniform sphere: (1) *There would be no sense in speaking of when the event occurred.* Because in a void in which nothing has existed or will ever exist there is no reference point in time, there would be no sense in speaking of when the event occurred; this would require the existence of other events to which reference could be made. The functioning of a watch or clock is the perfect example of a separate event which can provide an external standard of reference; the question 'when?' could then be answered by reference to 'the point at which the short hand was at 3 o'clock and the long hand was at 12 o'clock' for instance. Thus a solitary event in a void could have no temporal position (i.e., no position in time); for it would have no external temporal standard of reference – the question 'when?' would become meaningless. (2) *Time-wise, the event could not be said* *to be 'long' or 'short'*. In parallel to the previous consideration of temporal size we would require the existence of at least two events so that one can be described as longer or shorter in terms of the other. Otherwise the question 'how long' is meaningless.

Actual space and actual time have intrinsic relations to objects and events respectively, and thus we respectively define them: actual space is a matrix of objects; whilst actual time is a concatenation or chain of events. These definitions counter the ideas of actual space and actual time being continuities (i.e., uniform in the sense that a void is uniform) and as possessing existences independent of objects and events. One cannot deny that *mathematical space* and *mathematical time*, which are ideals, can possess such properties and have a valid use in allowing us to form a coherent picture of reality; but not actual space and actual time. Whereas mathematical space and time are systems we *abstract from* objects and events, actual space and actual time far from being abstractions from objects and events are constituted of them.

THE PHYSICAL–METAPHYSICAL DUALITY: MATTER AND VOID

The theory of the origin of the universe in current favour among scientists is the Superdense or 'Big Bang' theory. This has an earlier and a later form. In the earlier theory the universe evolved from one tiny superdense ball of matter which suffered a cataclysmic explosion. It was thought to be as a result of this that the universe is expanding. In this theory the universe was thought to have had a finite beginning and probably a finite ending. The theory currently in favour speculates that this expansion of the universe will one day stop and there will be a reversal whereby the universe contracts to become, once again, a superdense agglomeration of matter. This process of expansion and contraction is seen as a cycle without end or beginning. Apart from the ball of matter there is nothing, and implicit in these theories is an emptiness or void within which the ball of matter contracts and expands.

In the original theory scientists could not tell us 'where' the superdense ball of matter came from. The void in being beyond the physical is 'metaphysical'. The physical cannot be explained in terms of the metaphysical. It is therefore futile to ask the question 'where' the primeval ball of matter came from or the instant 'when' it came into being; because we would then be applying the categories of space, time and causation which necessarily belong to the physical, to beyond the physical. The logical difficulty might well have influenced some to opt for the perpetual, alternate contraction and expansion theory which escapes this problem because there is no beginning or end of time to consider.

No problem lies in unifying the African cosmological mythology with the superdense theories, although most myths point to a finite beginning to this material universe. When we recall Bambara accounts of creation which speak of a voice from the void bringing the world into being, or in the case of the Dogon, the first seed which contained in embryo everything which was to come into being we see a resemblance. Another version of the Dogon account given by the sage Ogotemmeli even goes as far as to speak of a primeval ball of clay squeezed by the one God, Amma,[14] and flung into space. This ball fragmented into pellets to form the stars.[15]

In the superdense theory it is also supposed that the common elements were formed from a single element, a primeval hydrogen. In this sense there exists a resemblance with ancient Egyptian and Dogon conceptions of eight elements or original ancestors evolving out of a primeval water.

From various texts the ancient Egyptian account of the creation can be understood as one in which the Demi-urge or Creator-God evolved himself out of the primeval water, Nu (or Nun) which he created* and thereafter set about the work of ordering the world, constituting it into eight elements thus, with himself included, forming the Ennead or company of Nine

* Theophile Obenga in his forthcoming book *African Philosophy during the period of the Pharaohs: 2780–330 B.C.*, believes the Egyptian primeval water, Nun, was uncreated. Please see appendix for my discussion of this.

Gods consisting of the Creator God (appearing in the forms of Atum (or Tmu), Kheperac (or Ra) and the gods Shu and Tefnut, Seb and Nut, Osiris and Isis, Seth and Nepthys.

The African account of creation is a striking analogy to the development of consciousness in the new born child as we can see: The development of a concept of the self and self awareness in the infant involves the young child extracting him/herself from the undifferentiated totality of his/her experience. For we may recall that the infant, in his first perceptions of the world, is unable to be aware of himself as distinct from all that he hears, sees, and feels about him. This image of the human consciousness emerging into a self distinct and yet emerging from the world is precisely that evoked by the account of the emergence of the Creator-God from the primeval water in African cosmology.

In the text, Nu has been identified as the void or nothingness. Nu (or Nun) is similar in sound to the Wolof word "Nen", which Diop, in comparing the two, translates as "nothingness".[16] Nu is the primeval water or primeval 'matter'. In previous passages these have been seen as being a symbolic veil for the supreme abstraction that is nothingness. In the *Book of Coming Forth by Day (Egyptian Book of the Dead)* the primeval 'matter', "paut", is often translated as being "unformed matter". The implication from this, is of a matter which has not yet come into existence. We will recall in previous passages defining the void objectively as the absence of an object; that is, the absence of matter. [17]

The primeval Nu is often associated with chaos (*isfet*), to the extent that several authors take care to dissociate them. However, the origin of order in ancient Egyptian cosmology is the creator-God whose actions established Maat, the principle of moral order, balance and reciprocity (that is, cause and effect). Chaos is merely the absence of order; before the Creator-God created himself and the universe, therefore, there must have been chaos. The forces of chaos are represented by the mythical serpent, Apophis, whose infinitely long body forms a bottomless abyss or void, forcing those he swallows into non-existence.

In ancient Egyptian texts, passages seem to imply that the primeval water was not literally water. In the *Book of the Dead* reference is made to 'celestial waters' or the 'watery abyss of the sky'. These terms, as translated, would appear to refer to space.

It was mentioned earlier that the primeval Nu should not be seen as an absolutely empty space; for Nu is not dead, but alive, endowed with a hidden creative force. Within the Nu exists a Divine Soul or Mind which had already designed all that would come into being. In the *Book of the Dead* it says:

> My name is Soul, creator of Nu, making his seat in the underworld. My nest is not seen, I have not cracked my egg.[18]

This passage clearly shows that within Nu the Divine Soul did not exist in any material form; only as an invisible potentiality. This aspect of the primeval Nu is symbolised by the egg; the symbol of the hidden creative power which is about to be unleashed.

The existence of the Divine Soul in Nu points to the Egyptian belief in the idea of a World-Soul, which they called *Ba* [19]. Its name indicates that this Soul also exists in human beings as their *ba*. It is like the idea of Brahman in Indian religion, which is the supreme all-inclusive Being of all existence. Brahman also has a personal aspect in Brahma-Atman, the Inner Self residing within each individual. This dual nature of a World-Soul is echoed in traditional African religion by the Igbo duality of Chi and Chukwu. The word Chukwu is really made up of two words 'Chi-Ukwu' meaning 'the Great Chi'. Chi is the root of the duality just as the root word in the Indian duality, Brahman and Brahma-Atman is Brahma. Brahma-Atman, however, corresponds to Chi and Brahma to Chukwu (Chi-Ukwu). Chukwu may be seen as an example of the all-encompassing aspect of the World-Soul in African traditional religion. Chi, the other part of the duality, is sometimes described as the spark of the Supreme Being which is in each individual and whereas Chukwu makes many possibilities available to the development of each life, it is the Chi that chooses from these possibilities to create each person's unique destiny.[20] In another striking resemblance to Asian religions we note that the Chi is thought to return to the all-encompassing aspect of Chukwu when a person dies.[21]

Above we see that ancient and traditional Africa, in a like manner to other cultures of the South, merged science, philosophy and religion into an integrated whole; one which is consistent with theories of (a) the evolution of the universe in modern physics and (b) the evolution of the self from the external universe in modern psychology. However, we must beware of studying African religion and philosophy solely in order to compare it with modern science; for one is then in danger of disregarding important differences whilst focusing on the similarities. African thought, like any other, can best be understood in its own right.

APPENDIX

DISCUSSION OF THEOPHILE OBENGA'S THESIS ON THE PRIMEVAL NUN

In his quest to find out what the ancient Egyptians had to say about the beginning of beginnings, Theophile Obenga, in his forthcoming book, *African Philosophy during the Period of the Pharaohs: 2780–330 B.C.* has translated some 27 texts or fragments of texts, some of which have been translated for the very first time by an African scholar.

From his translation of the Bremner Rhind Papyrus and other texts it is made evident that the Egyptians had a conception of the origin of the universe close to that of modern physics, which, as we have noted, holds that the universe evolved out of a primeval agglomeration of matter. Obenga compares this with an ancient Egyptian cosmology where he discerns that

> In the very beginning, before all the fundamental elements, before the Demi-urge or the Creator himself, there was *Nun*, posited as an abyssal matter, aqueous and vital, the Unique Substratum, the singular place of the plural emergence of the elements that form the universe, (that) totality of knowable reality. What is created comes out of what is uncreated, out of the agitation of an almost impalpable water. *Nun*, which is the ideogram of no anterior fate whatsoever, has no beginning.[1]

Though this author believes no amount of criticism can make any difference to the immense contribution Obenga has made to the understanding of ancient African philosophy, it must be said that there is evidence to suggest that the primeval Nu or Nun was indeed created; for in the Bremner Rhind Papyrus translated by Obenga the Lord of the Universe says:

> I made everything alone, before any being (other than myself) manifested itself to existence to act with me in these places. There I made forms of existence from the force (which is in me). There, I created Abyss (still) dormant and not having found a place to stand up yet.[2]

The Bremner Rhind Papyrus is remarkably similar in its reasoning and philosophical language to the Papyrus of Nesi Amsu as translated by E.A. Wallis Budge. In this text the Lord of the Universe records:

> I evolved by the evolution of evolutions. I evolved myself under the form of the evolutions of the god Khepera, which were evolved at the beginning of all time. I evolved with the evolutions of the god Khepera; I evolved by the evolution of evolutions - that is to say, I developed myself from the primeval matter which I made, I developed myself out of the primeval matter.[3]

In the *Book of the Dead*, it says of the creator-God:-

> ... (Thou art) the One god who came into being in the beginning of time. Thou didst create the earth, thou didst fashion man, thou didst make the watery abyss of the sky [4]

And other statements made in the *Book of the Dead* point to the creation of Nu:-

> I have brought myself into being together with Nu in my name of Khepera.[5]
> My name is Soul, Creator of Nu ...[6]

The following is an important passage from Chapter 17 of the *Book of the Dead* as translated by Obenga:-

> I am Atum when I am the One to exist being alone in Nun, and I am Ra when he rises in glory, when he commands and governs. Who is this? - It is Ra. I am the great god who

came into existence out of himself, the water, Nun, father of the gods.[7]

The above passage might be read as identifying the Creator-God with the primeval matter, Nu. We note that the Creator-God first of all exists alone as Atum in the primeval Nu; when he rises out of the primeval water he becomes Ra, the demiurge ready to create the universe. Thus when the proclamation is made: 'I am the great god who came into existence out of himself, the water, Nu, father of the gods' it is Ra who speaks, identifying himself with the primeval Nun.

A further argument against the anteriority of the Nun to the Creator-God is the observation that the Creator-God is believed to have created even existence itself. It follows from this that nothing could have existed before existence itself and hence the creator. It was noted early on that in ancient Egyptian texts, God's essence is existence:-

When I manifested myself to existence, existence began to exist.[8]

In the papyrus of Nesi Amsu we will recall the Lord of the Universe proclaiming:-

I evolved the evolving of evolutions ...

All this leaves us a circular image of a Creator-God who evolved himself out of a primeval matter which he created. There is left only the implication of an infinite cycle. The image of the self-created Creator evokes the African symbol of the snake with its tale in its mouth. We note that this very symbol (often used by the ancient Egyptians with the body of Osiris in place of the serpent) occurs in the illustration of the god Nu rising out of the primeval water.[9]

Part III

ETHICS AND MORAL EXPERIENCE

1.
GOOD AND EVIL

The Supreme Good, the Summum Bonum we wrongly attributed to Aristotle, is the personal Idea humans choose to have of God. But this is God as the personified Absolute, not the impersonal Absolute which is neither good nor evil.

George James notes that for the ancient Egyptians, this Supreme Good 'is equated with both happiness and knowledge. This ... is a well-being which is conditioned by good action. This is an attainment in which man becomes god-like through self-denial of external needs and the cultivation of the mind: for happiness comes not through the perishable things of the external world, but through the things which endure, which are within us'.[1]

The Supreme Good is equated with happiness and James goes on to say that the hedonists marked a departure, along with Aristotle, from this definition.[2] It seems that at one period in history the ancient Africans defined the Supreme Good as happiness; then at a later period, the Greeks (who then became the dominant culture) defined it as pleasure. However, the Egyptians did not condemn pleasure, as is evidence by the continuation of corporeal enjoyment in the mythology of the underworld.[3] One would have good reason to place their priorities in this order. For the pursuit of happiness is surely the chief of human pursuits. Even if one pursues pleasure to its limit, this is surely a vain attempt to sustain fleeting and delusive moments of happiness. In addition to this most of us know from experience than an obsession with pleasure is rarely conducive to happiness. There is a point beyond which pleasure ceases to be. Happiness on the other hand is a more durable state of mind. We begin to see that happiness and pleasure are quite different things. Whereas pleasure results from an interaction with some definite object; happiness is a state of well-being not derived from any particular object in the world, but is experienced as a result of a total overview of one's life and its possibilities. Whereas pleasure is related to the love of worldly things, happiness can only stem from a love of life as a whole.

Even in morality we find the African principle of opposites to be operative. Though God is thought of as the essence of goodness and the source of all good, God is also, indirectly, the source of all evil; for by the principle of opposites, His(Her) goodness causes evil to come into being, since goodness has no meaning if evil does not also exist. Says one Ashanti priest: 'God created the possibility of evil in the world. God has created the knowledge of good and evil in every person and allowed him to choose his way'.[4]

The final comment made by the Ashanti priest above confronts us with the question of whether the concepts of 'good' and 'evil' are known by intuition or through experience. Intuitive moral principles or laws seem unlikely human possessions. If such principles or laws were intuitively known our experience of moral obligation could surely have no reference to worldly experience (i.e., sensation and emotion). Moral law would have to be apprehended with equal weight on the conscience regardless of the situation in which the moral agent happened to find him/herself. It is not difficult to point out instances to the contrary. If a man is in a situation where he is forced to take the life of another, it can be almost taken for granted that his conscience would weigh heavier over the killing of a friend than an enemy. His conscience would weigh less upon him still if his victim is an enemy not encountered on a personal level. The executive head of state who orders that innocent civilians be bombed in the course of fighting a war, is not physically confronted with the human expense of his decision. He is unlikely to experience the same crisis of conscience as the pilots or foot soldiers who execute his decisions. Comparing the situations of decision maker and executer, can it be held that a moral agent found in each of these situations would in each case apprehend his moral obligation with equal force? If one accepts that conscience weighs heaviest upon the executer, one must also concede that moral obligation is somehow related to worldly experience and is therefore unlikely to derive from the intuition.

It is possible to imagine that our notions of good and evil stem respectively from experiences to which we react positively and negatively, approving or disapproving of them. For instance we react positively to pleasure and negatively to pain; we react positively to a show of kindness and negatively to a show of hostility, etc. If anything is given to us prior to experience, it is the mechanism to produce these responses. On examination, however, we see that this ability to discriminate does *not* constitute knowledge in the form of concepts or principles. This is not to say our responses to moral situations are wholly instinctive. Often, it is after the initial internal response to a situation, which may be one of approval or disapproval, that a conscious choice is made as to how one should actively respond. Despite the complexities of moral situations one can assume quite confidently, I believe, that our instinctive reactions to pain must be at the core of what we regard to be evil. This may perhaps be viewed as simplistic. But the aim is merely to point out the essentials of moral theory, not to formulate it. In any case, in respect of the creation of a theory of morals simplicity is an important guideline. Over-complexed moral theories are here viewed with distrust; for the more complex a moral theory, the less universally applicable it must be. The value of a moral theory must rest in the degree to which it is universally applicable regardless of culture. Surely there is no experience which we can identify so universally with evil as that of pain when this is inflicted on person by person. This must be the simplest starting point.

It is through our own personal experience of pain that we are able to appreciate the pain of others. This must be the basis of our moral consciousness in relation to the treatment of others. Without the personal experience we have no yardstick with which to empathise with the sufferings of others or which we could use to extrapolate in trying to understand their situation. One might ask what it is, fundamentally, that makes us see ourselves in the place of others. All that will be said is that it is surely no more than the extension of the response mechanism to pain in ourselves, except that it is now to some extent enveloped in a consciousness and deliberacy where one places oneself in the shoes of the sufferer and 'feels' his or her pain. From the innate response to my own pain I am able to find a response to the pain of others.

In our discussion of good and evil we might note that the world is not really as straight forward as the discussion might so far imply. We have demonstrated that our notions of good and evil must come from our experience. Yet human experience is diverse; traditional institutions function to unite this diversity in each society. In this sense, religion has been fundamental in providing the moral fabric of society. Our senses of moral obligation, our senses of right and wrong are moulded by the norms, values and beliefs of the society in which we are nurtured. In a sense, therefore, ethics are culturally relative. But in saying this a distinction needs to be made between rules and principles of ethics. It is possible to point out ethical principles which are universal to all societies; for instance, the ethical principle that human life is an end in itself. But ethical rules (i.e., the manner in which a society complies with ethical principle) vary from one society to the next.

Nkrumah makes this distinction in *Consciencism*. He sees principles as being more general and permanent; whereas rules refer to the manner in which the principle must be applied.[5] An example of this might be taken by considering any topic about which public opinion is likely to vary from one society to another. For instance, abortion. The ethical principle involved here is that human life is an end in itself; but the controversy rests on what a society defines as 'human life'. If the law of one land proclaims abortion to be murder, this is an ethical rule particular to that society; for in another society, the foetus may not be considered to have the status of human life. In such a case, the mother is the only human life concerned and though abortion may be accepted on this basis the principle on which it is accepted in the latter society is the same principle on which it is rejected in the former.

In Africa, we must not fail to take account of the imposition of foreign culture and the consequences this has had for the development of our ethics. The result has been confusion arising from the clash, in some aspects, of radically opposed cultures. Take, as an instance, the conflict brought about by the co-existence of the extended family system and European industrial culture. Malaises which have resulted from this, such as nepotism and petty corruption, do not have the same moral significance in Africa as they do in Europe; that is, they are not taken as seriously. In a society where employment is scarce and social welfare non-existent, there are few breadwinners and the individual is forced to choose, not between right and wrong, but between an evil and a lesser evil. When the well-being of the family depends on the ability of perhaps a single breadwinner to provide, which is the greater evil; a dishonest transaction or a hungry family?

Just as the world is inherently neither good nor evil, so is the human being. A person is only good or evil insofar as his/her actions are judged as such. When we talk of good we need to make a distinction between acts of good and the inherent quality of goodness. The difference between inherent goodness and goodness in human action is central to what Mbiti calls the African concept of morality. He says that African morality '... is a morality of "conduct" rather than a morality of "being". This is what one might call dynamic ethics rather than static ethics, for it defines what a person *does* rather than what he *is*. Conversely, a person is what he is because of what he does, rather than he does what he does because of what he is. Kindness is not a virtue unless someone is kind; murder is not evil until someone kills .... Man is not by nature either "good" or "bad" except in terms of what he does or does not do'.[6] Thus African morality defines good and evil solely in terms of human action; they are not seen as having existence independent of human beings.

2.
FREEDOM AND MORAL RESPONSIBILITY

FREEWILL AND DETERMINISM

Why should the subject of freedom be so vital to the study of ethics and morality? Quite obviously, without freedom of will we could not choose between good and evil and therefore could not possess moral responsibility. If I am seen by others as having done a good deed, this is not enough. For it to be a truly good deed it must have been my intention, my choice to do good.

African religions do not appear to doubt man and woman's freedom as Western philosophy has done due to the conceived conflict between freewill and the principle of cause and effect. The Western preoccupation with science and technology seems to have led many towards a mechanistic view of the world in which freewill and natural law are seen as incompatible, and in which, as a result, human freedom is denied existence and thought illusory. Why, we shall see shortly; but we first of all need to see how this conflict is conceived. Take the standard example of the policeman on the point of deciding whether or not to accept a bribe in return for turning a blind eye on an offender. On the one hand we would suppose he has the freedom to accept or reject the bribe, and should he accept it we would hold him morally responsible. On the other, seeing things mechanistically, every mental and physical state he happens to be in is determined by his preceding mental and physical states. Hence, even if he seemed to take the bribe 'deliberately' we cannot hold him morally responsible; for we would eventually realise that the cause of his present mental and physical states precede even the time of his birth. This absolves him of moral responsibility altogether, which probably seems absurd. Thus we have a conflict; is the agent free or determined by the principle of cause and effect?

African philosophy appears to see freedom and natural law as compatible. This harmony is implied by the ancient African concept, personified by the Goddess *Maat*, in which physical and moral order are seen to co-exist. Maat is simultaneously physical and ethical justice. They may be seen to co-exist by distinguishing between a subjective and objective human viewpoint; between the spiritual and physical aspects of human nature. The subjective is the viewpoint from which the individual is the observer upon his own actions, evaluating them in terms of the purpose he gives them. From this viewpoint he is undoubtedly free to define his life as he wishes. He understands his life as regulated by the purpose he gives his actions as opposed to their causes, and the need to see them in terms of chemistry and physics does not arise. This viewpoint is obviously private and exclusive; no other person could ever behold it. This subjective realm of the individual, the agent, is therefore a closed universe. On the other hand, the objective viewpoint is that in which the agent's actions are observed by the onlooker; it is the onlooker's viewpoint. The onlooker is not capable of evaluating the agent's actions in terms of the purpose the agent has given them, but only as effects and causes. The onlooker is forever shut out from the agent's impenetrable world. The agent's actions are not seen in isolation from the environment; the agent is part of the social and natural environment, acting upon it and suffering its action.

RECOGNISING MAN AND WOMAN AS ENDS IN THEMSELVES

Thus the observed conflict between freedom and natural law is the result of oblivion to man and woman's dual nature. With the retention of freedom, man and woman also retain their intrinsic worth; they remain ends within themselves, having a value which cannot be measured in material terms. The exercise of freedom is that which distinguishes human beings from automatons. By denying human freedom the Western mechanistic worldview, by implication, devalues human worth. As opposed to being ends in themselves people become means to greater ends in a hierarchy. In the viewpoint of tyrannous powers, people become mere tools, expendable once their usefulness is ended. But from their own perspectives they remain ends in themselves.

We are led to an apparent difficulty. I as the subject can attribute freedom and intrinsic value to myself; but I as the onlooker see the other as the determined outcome of his circumstances. From my point of view as the onlooker, it seems the other has no freedom. He is therefore not an end. However, at the same time as being an onlooker, I am also a subject and experience my own personal sense of freedom and self worth. It is necessarily through my own experience that I must view the position of the other. I see the other as a human being like myself and I am morally bound to infer that the other also has freedom and that transcendent value we ascribe to human beings. Through my own personal experience of these I am able to respect these qualities in the other.

Though my own freedom and sense of self worth are experienced immediately and are therefore always real for me, the freedom and non-material worth of the other cannot be considered to exist in every situation and is really a moral Idea which functions in maintaining a moral order in the world. The self is the measure of the other and naturally, every person considers him/herself an end; no material cost is too great a price to save one's own flesh. The other is considerable as an end in himself until his behaviour becomes predatory and he poses a threat to human life. At this point he is no longer seen as an essentially valuable being, but as an object which threatens life and is expendable in the interest of survival. The predator becomes a threat to human life at the point where he no longer recognises the other's freedom and right to exist.

Looking at the above problem from another angle, Fanon identifies mutual recognition in human relationships as inseparable from respect. On this thesis, which he derives from Hegel, he says: 'Man is human only to the extent to which he tries to impose his existence on another man in order to be recognised by him. As long as he has not been effectively recognised by the other, that other will remain the theme of his actions. It is on that other being, on recognition by that other being that his human worth and reality depend'.[1] We must remember that Fanon makes this statement in the context of colonial and racial domination where the European power structure controls the means of production of the entire black world. This is the critical and quintessential case of the denial of freedom and humanity of one human being by another. In the context of the present discussion the recognition of which Fanon speaks is the recognition of the freedom and humanity of one human being by another. Without this recognition by the other, these values remain purely subjective, existing only in the mind of the individual. In order that my freedom and humanity be recognised and therefore objectified I must reach out from the confines of my personal world and make plain my demands for recognition by the other, even at the risk of conflict.[2] This would not have been necessary had the other not had power over my very means of survival. Because freedom is that which makes man and woman ends in themselves, human beings and not tools, it cannot be compromised in the face of violence.

COLLECTIVE OR CORPORATE MORAL RESPONSIBILITY

We have already noted that in traditional Africa moral responsibility is a corporate affair with the community being responsible for the conduct of its individual members. Similarly, a wrong done to the individual is a wrong inflicted on his/her whole community. African morality recognises that we do not exist alone in the world and appears to see a concrete link among beings. We can very easily relate this philosophy to the world in which we live today; and we find that Fanon was a modern exponent of this traditional African theme, even if unwitting. He says: 'I cannot dissociate myself from the future that is proposed for my brother. Every one of my acts commits me as a man. Every one of my silences, every one of my cowardices reveals me as a man'.[3] His belief in collective moral responsibility is made even plainer from this quotation which he borrows from Karl Jaspers: '... there exists among men, because they are men, a solidarity through which each shares a responsibility for every injustice and every wrong committed in the world'.[4]

Fanon's outlook differs from Jasper's, however, in that Fanon, as a black man, had no misgivings of a universal brotherhood of man (I presume he does not exclude women), although he did aspire to the eventual emergence of one. Fanon believed that within the human community allegiances are forged and a polarization exists along the lines of race first and foremost. Thus when Fanon speaks of his brothers, he is referring to his African brothers. In Fanon's colonial Africa, therefore, there are two distinct communities: that of the native African and the European settler.

Through this idea of corporate or collective moral responsibility, we begin to understand Fanon's standpoint on violence.[5] The settler community is collectively responsible for the brutality of its police force and the denial of the African's rights. Even to be silent is to collude with the forces of injustice. Seen in this light, no member of the settler community could be absolved of guilt unless he actively opposes the actions of his people.

In speaking of corporate moral responsibility, the concept as it occurs in African philosophy cannot be fully understood without one knowing who constitute the community in African society. The community in African society includes those dead (our ancestors), those living and those yet to be born.[6] This inevitably reveals the fundamentally *ecological* nature of African ethics. The African way of life is to live in harmony with nature through avoiding disturbance of the ecological balance. The fact that the community includes those yet to be born means the individual must act bearing in mind the consequences which may befall future generations as a result of his or her action. Thus, for instance, it would be against the African code of ethics to destroy too many trees for firewood leaving too few to provide fuel, shade, and other forms of protection for our children's children. It would be against the code to dispose of toxic wastes in the rivers from which our children's children will be forced to drink, and so on. In contrast, the western idea of community is restricted to those who live here and now. This discontinuity of past, present and future and isolation of the living from antiquity and posterity in terms of moral responsibility could have something to do with western society's wastefulness, recklessness and ecological irresponsibility.

It is true that the African code of ethics in regard to ecology is being violated in virtually every country on the continent today through deforestation, the hunting of rare animals for their skins or ivory, etc. However, these violations result from the fact that African economies have been tailored to suit the demands of the Western market. The influence of capitalism on the African continent has been to draw Africans further and further away from traditional modes of life which necessitated living in harmony with the natural environment. The choice is often between the doing away with tradition and starvation, due to the fact that it is made impossible for Africans to live outside the neo-colonial set-up. The over-tapping of rubber trees is another example of the violation of the ecological balance. In the Belgian Congo in the times of King Leopold, for instance, Africans had a hand amputated if they failed to meet the rubber quota demanded by their colonial masters. Colonialism destroyed the systems which enabled the traditional means of livelihood to thrive; and the African today has, in most cases, no means of survival other than through the sale of his/her labour to the prevailing, inherently anti-ecological, capitalist system.

MORAL CONDUCT

'Do unto others as you would have others do unto you'. Encapsulated in this advice is the moral attitude we know all men and women ought to have towards one another. It contains, better than any command which comes to mind, the entire sphere of individual conduct towards others. The origin of this wisdom might have been thought Christian; but in the Egyptian

Book of Khun Anup we find its earlier form: 'Redress is short but misfortune is long and a good deed returns to those who do it. This is the precept: Do to the doer that he or she may also do'.[7] Plainly this is a precept understood in all cultures, but in Africa it is often the first word of warning to one who behaves badly towards those about him. In a Swahili folktale we learn how Sadaka, the youngest of seven sons travels to an island inhabited by a ruthless king in order to free his brothers who have all been imprisoned on the island. But before doing so he loads his boat with millet, rice and cattle which he uses to feed the starving birds, flies and jinns he encounters on his trips to three different islands before reaching the island of the ruthless king. In return, the birds, flies and jinns each offer him incense to be burned whenever he wished to call for their help in the future. On reaching the island of the ruthless king he eventually finds himself in a position where he must pass three tests set by the king. If he fails any one of them he will die. But if he passes them he will be able to marry the king's daughter. He survives the ordeal only because he is able to call upon the assistance of those he had helped in the past.[8]

Kant in his Categorical Imperative says something very similar to the above biblical precept although more obscure: 'Act as if the maxim of your action were to become, through your will, a universal law of nature'. In other words, do as you would wish everybody universally to do.

In all the various forms of this precept we find the concern for others balanced by the concern for self. In this we see the perfect example of the ancient African principle of *Maat* in operation. In all cases the obligation to do good is balanced and supported by the sanction that if one does not, then this doing or failure to do will surely return to them in the form of harsh treatment or neglect by others in one's moment of need. We see the comparison and connection between the self and others to be vital in the sense that it is on the basis of our personal experience that we are able to respect the individual rights of others.

The ethical precepts which have been presented can never serve as perfect guides to moral conduct, for human nature seems too complex to be constrained totally by them. It seems that no matter how one tries to formulate universally applicable ethical rules, there will always be an exception to a rule. Like the laws of science, the laws of ethics cannot be absolute; although the principles remain the same.

Nkrumah, in expounding his philosophy of Consciencism, explains that the ethics of his philosophy are founded on a study of the nature of man. He says that Kant (despite grounding his ethics in the principle that man is an end in himself as, likewise, Consciencism does) had forbidden ethics to be founded on a study of man.[9] In this sense, it would seem that many of the problems with progress in ethics might be attributed to this Kantian mentality. It would be nice to believe that the human being is essentially good by nature; but history shows that just as human beings have immense capacity for doing good, they possess an equal capacity for evil. Ideally we would be happy to follow all righteous ethical rules if these were followed universally; for we sense within ourselves that the spirit of these rules is correct. However, when these rules are not obeyed universally, we continue to abide by them, in some cases, at our own peril. History shows this and it is because of this that we must go along with Nkrumah in founding our ethics, not on idealist conceptions of the goodness of human beings, but on our observation of the nature of human beings. Let us take, for example, the commandment 'thou shalt not kill'. This rule is happily followed as long as it is universally abided by everyone. This is obviously an ideal situation. In the present reality it is not followed by all and it has become a law which forbids the victim of aggression the right of self defence; for effective self defence often involves armed struggle.

In reality, violence needs to be qualified. Not only are there many forms of violence other than physical violence, but we cannot in real life dissociate violence from the reason for violence. Violence is rarely, if ever, an end in itself. Often it is used to take possession of people or things; conversely it may be the only means of self-defence. Now we cannot justify violence which puts things before people. We cannot justify the violence which facilitates the domination of some people by others. But what of the violence used to end this domination and restore a moral order? Here we come to the crux of the problem many have with non-violence. For non-violence appears to rely upon some external arbiter of the moral law above human beings. The reason why the above commandment denies human beings the right to redress the moral balance is because God is implicitly supposed as the sole arbiter of the moral law. Man and woman are therefore disqualified from taking the law into their own hands. They are not qualified to judge for all judgement is left to God. It might appear that the opponent of non-violence does not place his/her trust in God to restore the moral order among us. But this is not so and it would be wrong for us to believe the opponent of non-violence to be necessarily an atheist. He or she may conceive that although God exists as the ground of our reality, God does not exist as a human being and cannot therefore be associated with such human acts as listening, speaking, etc., or, in this case, judging, unless this is through human beings themselves. Thus, the oppressed by retaliating in self-defence, have not made the final judgement. For, in this sense, God and history may be seen as one in determining the final outcome.

Fundamental to the way in which we treat others is the way in which we see ourselves and discipline ourselves. The human being is driven by desires both on a spiritual level and on a material one, in accordance with his or her dual nature. On the spiritual level there is the quest to achieve high ideals; while on the material level there is the quest for pleasure. In order to realise our complete natures as simultaneously spiritual and physical beings it is necessary that we discover the balance between these aspects of ourselves so that one is not pursued excessively to the detriment of the other. In this vein the ancient Africans of Egypt pursued the Ten Virtues of Eternal Happiness. These, James claims, were the original ten from which Plato plagiarised his four cardinal virtues of *Justice, Fortitude, Prudence* and *Temperance*:[10]

1. Control of thought.
2. Control of action.
3. Steadfastness of purpose.
4. Identity with the spiritual life or higher ideals.

5. Evidence of having a mission in life.
6. Evidence of a call to spiritual orders or the priesthood.
7. Freedom from resentment when under persecution and wrong.
8. Confidence in the power of the master as teacher.
9. Confidence in one's own ability to learn.
10. Readiness or preparedness for initiation.

The Egyptians conceived of virtue as a union of opposites in which our spiritual and physical aspects come together to exist harmoniously.[11] This implies moderation in the pursuit of our dual nature rather than a severe asceticism. True inner peace must lie in discovering our unique personal balance between these pursuits and being disciplined enough to maintain this. This in turn requires self knowledge or self awareness of our individual limitations and affinities for worldly things.

James, in explaining the goal of the Egyptian Mystery System, writes: 'The earliest theory of salvation is the Egyptian Theory. The Egyptian Mystery System had as its most important object, the deification of man, and taught that the soul of man if liberated from its bodily fetters, could enable him to become godlike and see the Gods in this life and attain the beatific vision and hold communion with the immortals (Ancient Mysteries, C.H. Vail, p.25)'.[12]

He also notes that Plotinus had described this experience as the liberation of the mind from its finite consciousness to become one with the Infinite. Also, as a liberation from the wheel of reincarnation, of continual death and rebirth.[13]

In traditional African religion the belief in reincarnation seems to have evolved or become modified. We do not find the cycle of rebirth which is to be broken through great effort. Furthermore, reincarnation remains within the family line and the child inherits traits of a foreparent rather than the entire personality.[14]

In traditional Africa there remains, however, something akin to the ancient African idea of the liberation of the finite individual consciousness into a cosmic consciousness; for Segy notes that the key to the traditional African way of life is the 'dissolution of the individual into the collective consciousness'.[15] There are, it seems several levels of this 'collective consciousness'. On the most concrete level this is the collective consciousness of the immediate human community. But in Africa human beings are only one part of a community that includes the animals, the plants and all of nature. Thus there also exists a cosmic level of collective consciousness in the traditional African philosophy.

Although interesting to us, it is not enough to leave African moral precepts in their historical context without looking at their relevance to our present. Of the Egyptian Virtues of Eternal Happiness we must ask: What meaning does the ancient African system of virtues have for us today? Looking at the ten virtues, some of them are evidently inapplicable as they relate to the neophytes of the Egyptian Mystery School. But whatever we may think of Plato's plagiarism, his Four Cardinal Virtues condense the originals into a form more applicable to the modern lifestyle:

(i) Justice

Under Justice, according to G.G.M. James, we can place the virtues of the control of thought and the control of action. Our actions determine the type of people we are; but prior to our actions are our thoughts. There are three levels on which human beings are able to exercise their wills: thought, speech and action, in order of increasing concreteness and severity. Plainly it is wrong to think badly of another without reasonable cause; worse still to speak badly of them and even worse still to cause them actual physical harm. Though we are morally judged by what we do and say, what we think ultimately determines what we become and what we do and say. If we wish to avoid the things we habitually do and say we must begin by changing our habitual patterns of thought. This requires great presence of mind and continual vigilance and alertness to our own thoughts to be able to replace negative thoughts with positive ones when they arise. The notion of justice in relation to the control of thought and action would appear to relate to the natural manner in which fortunate circumstances eventually follow from righteous action which is the result of positive thought; whilst unfortunate circumstances follow from unrighteous acts which result from negative thoughts. We might learn from the first two verses of the Buddhist Dhammapada:

1. Our life is shaped by our mind; we become what we think. Suffering follows an evil thought as the wheels of a cart follow the oxen that draw it.

2. Our life is shaped by our mind; we become what we think. Joy follows a pure thought like a shadow that never leaves.

(ii) Temperance

According to James, temperance is the meaning of the virtue of identity with the spiritual life or the higher ideals. Temperance refers to the control of the desire for the material in the sense that man and woman must cultivate the desire for the spiritual life or the higher ideals in order to maintain the balance and the harmony of their spiritual and material natures. Excessive love of material things saps that part of our vital energy that belongs to the pursuit of the spiritual or the higher ideals. The ultimate spiritual ideal held by the ancient Africans, the Summom Bonum attributed to Aristotle, is happiness.

The pursuit of happiness involves the conflict between the desire for material pleasures and the desire to achieve spiritual or higher ideals. Imbalance in the level at which these are pursued leads eventually to unhappiness. Life is thus a tension between the spiritual and material.

(iii) Fortitude

Fortitude is equivalent to the virtue of steadfastness of purpose. This relates to our resolve to rise above adverse situations. This is strengthened by a firm belief in a purpose to one's life.

The purpose of human existence in African philosophy is given by the concept of continuity of past, present and future. Plainly and simply the purpose of the living is to carry on from where our ancestors have left off and to pave the way for those yet to be born.

(iv) Prudence

According to James, the virtue of a deep insight into nature is equivalent to prudence. This relates to our understanding of ourselves, the community in which we exist and the environment – all of these being intimately interrelated.

AFTERWORD

Despite a common cultural past, Africa today is a continent of religious, ideological, ethnic and linguistic diversity. In part, this has been due to the migrations and separate development of Africans over the ages. But to a greater extent it is a diversity born of a long history of foreign influence.

Ancient Egyptian civilization which was the culmination of the rise of a Nile Valley culture that began in Kush, (ancient Ethiopia) fell as a result of numerous foreign (non-African) invasions. This spate of invasions beginning in about 671 B.C.[1] and involving the Assyrians, the Persians, the Greeks and the Romans was the first stage in the descent of African civilizations. The Greek and Roman invasions led to the destruction of the foundation of Egyptian high-culture, its education system. This destruction culminated with the edict by the Roman emperor, Justinian in 4 A.D., closing all of the mystery schools in Egypt and proclaiming Christianity as the state religion.[2] Thereafter, Egypt continued to be invaded by the Arabs, then the Turks, the French, and finally the British.[3] The character of Egyptian society has thus been greatly transformed, and one cannot today expect to find there, the descendants of its original inhabitants, who were pushed further south.[4]

However, the most devastating of set-backs to Africa has been as a result of the slavery, colonialism and neo-colonialism of the past 400 years. Foreign contact has drastically transformed Africa religiously, politically, economically and socially. Through the slave trade the African was uprooted and transported to the world's centres of production. Industrialization on the continent led to the severance of the sacred bond which existed between the African and his land, the traditional source of his livelihood. The African had to leave the rural areas to go and eke out a living for himself and his family in the urban centres. Consequently, the family, the nucleus of African social structure, began to disintegrate, as did the social structure itself. We were not helped by foreign systems of governance which served to divide us along linguistic lines. The African, severed from his land and his past, was flung into the contradictions of the townships, where two cultures fought.

The migration of Africans to the urban centres of the colonies and the breaking of the tie with the land, marked the beginning of a period in which Europe was to mould the African economy to its liking. It involved a shift, through coercion, in the application of African labour. Whereas before Africans farmed their land for their own sustenance; now they were creating wealth for the European through the extraction of raw materials and the farming of cash crops. These, of course, were exported to Europe.

Cabral identified the change in the mode of production (that is, the use of labour), the usurping of its control and the arrest of its unfettered development as crucial in the underdevelopment of Africa. Particularly, Cabral noted how this change had altered African culture:

> the change in the mode of production and its control has, through altering the material or economic relationships in the society, also altered its political and social relationships. It has altered the society's course of history and also culture.[5]

Nkrumah, in realising this, defined the task of his philosophy of Consciencism accordingly:

'Consciencism is the map in intellectual terms of the disposition of forces which will enable African society to digest the Western and the Islamic and the Euro-christian elements in Africa, and develop them in such a way that they fit into the African personality .... Philosophical consciencism is that philosophical standpoint which taking its start from the present content of the African conscience indicates the way out of which progress is forged out of the conflict in that conscience'.[6]

In defining the task of Consciencism, Nkrumah has laid out the task that lies ahead of us, even today. This is, the unification of our present diversities. The African personality has changed. It has adopted conflicting traits which are here to stay with us, at least for the meanwhile. Indeed, it seems that the best we can aspire towards in the immediate future is the forging of progress out of our differences. In order to do this we must emphasize that which we have in common: our cultural heritage.

This is not to say that we should be content with celebrating the glories of the African past without thought of progress. Rather, the African cultural heritage is the firm ground from which we should operate, the springboard for the advance of our arts, sciences and ethics in a manner consistent with the universal aspects of African culture.

I have tried to look at all of these areas of the African worldview as a holistic system in which they are interrelated. In opposition to this, the anti-holistic view of the Western world has as its basic manifestations the polarization of opposites which should naturally exist in harmony, the alienation of the individual and the estrangement of ethics and morality from the development and application of knowledge. We need to be aware of these in order to avoid mimicking them.

THE POLARIZATION OF OPPOSITES

The division and polarization of opposites in Western thought concerns the alienation of the spiritual and material aspects of human beings from each other, the division of human beings into those peoples who are emotional and those who are rational. These divisions seem to have been concretised or personalised in the polarization of the sexes in one case, and the polarization or division between so-called 'civilized' and 'primitive' peoples in the other. Does not Western society sometimes promote the ideas that women are intuitive or spiritual whilst men are more physical or materialistic; that women are more emotional whilst men are more rational? To ask these questions is not to deny that these traits do not exist as a result of our conditioning by the social environment, but merely to bring attention to the lines along which divisions have emerged. It can be argued that especially in the case of man/woman relationships, women do generally yearn more towards spiritual fulfilment whilst the fulfilment men pursue is more often physical. However, when it suits male intellectual 'authority' to do so the converse of this is also argued. At such times spirituality has become a virtue to be valued highly. For instance, Bachofen, in speculating that at one time all peoples of the earth existed under matriarchal systems (i.e., line of descent passing through the female) hails the coming of patriarchy as the ascension to a superior system representing '... above all spirituality, light, reason and delicacy'.[7]

These same divisions between spirituality and materialism, emotion and reason have been concretised through the division between so-called 'civilized' and 'primitive' peoples. Says Okpewho: 'A second shade of opinion concedes that life in traditional societies has a superabundance of the emotional as against the rational; the worldview is dominated by images which have their origins almost solely in man's uncharted sensations and are coloured more by mystical awe than by the confidence of reason'.[8] As Okpewho notes, some of the most ardent supporters of this view have come from the African continent, chief among whom was Leopold Senghor who became notorious for proclaiming that emotion is African as reason is Greek.

In regard to the association of materialism with 'primitive' peoples and spirituality with 'civilized' peoples, the following words of arch-racist Comte de Gobineau, speaking in the 19th century, reveal his association of materialism (in the sense of a greed for sensual pleasures) with the character of black people:

'The black variety is the lowest and lies at the bottom of the ladder .... Many of the senses are developed with a vigour unknown in the other two races: principally taste and smell. It is precisely in the greed for sensations that the most striking mark of its inferiority is found ...'.[9]

This attitude is echoed by such authors as Frazer in the *Golden Bough* and Budge in *Gods of the Egyptians*. The latter, having defined the Egyptians as fundamentally an African people, goes on to deny that any African peoples (and hence the Egyptians) could ever become meta-physicians.[10]

Throughout the first part of this work (*Being and Becoming*) it was stressed that the world in African philosophy is essentially of a dual spiritual-material nature. But Western society has alienated the spiritual from the material (through science and technology) and the material from the spiritual (through religion). This is shown by the acute polarization of science and religion. The alienation of the spiritual from the material is encountered in Western science where science cannot go beyond the purely material description of things. Consequently, the question of the fundamental or 'Ultimate Cause' of motion does not arise, leaving unbridged the gulf that lies between science and religion. This is not the case in the African worldview where beliefs in regard to the nature and behaviour of matter are embodied within the religious system. Thus the fundamental or 'Ultimate Cause' can without conflict be attributed to an All-pervading or Universal Life-Force.

The alienation of the material aspect of human beings from the spiritual aspect of human beings probably resulted from the Stoic and early Euro-christian belief that spiritual development is independent of material well-being.[11] It is through this idea, now recurring among modern fundamentalist christians, that the individual is urged to pursue his or her own salvation whilst social injustices are practically neglected; being thought to hold no consequences for spiritual development. Thus we have the situation where fundamentalists are able to claim that what the black people of South Africa need today is not so much liberation from racist oppression as spiritual liberation.

A further symptom of spiritual and material alienation manifests itself in the polarization of art and science. Western society has separated the arts and the sciences as being incompatible bed-mates, identifying them respectively with emotion and reason. However, we have already seen that the process of creativity in the sciences is not purely and exclusively rational; nor is it in the arts purely and exclusively emotional.

The discussion of the polarization of the sexes is of course one of dominance of men over women. The present world is in a state of almost universal patriarchy. According to Diop in *Cultural Unity of Black Africa*, this has not always been the case in the Southern Hemisphere where civilizations were originally matriarchal. This matriarchy was a natural state of harmony between the sexes as opposed to the domination of one by the other. Diop's theory puts forward that patriarchy characterised the cultures of the Northern Hemisphere and that through conquest patriarchy was imposed on other matriarchal cultures. In Africa, the imposition of patriarchy is traced, by Diop, to the incursion of Islam.[12]

Ifi Amadiume in her work on the matriarchal foundations of Igbo society, supports Diop's thesis but differs in not accepting that there existed a 'harmonious dualism' between men and women or, as Diop claims, a corporate co-existence of matriarchal and patriarchal systems.[13]

Though one may reserve serious criticisms of this work one has to acknowledge the importance of the issues addressed in Andree Collard's (assisted by Joyce Contrucci) *Rape of the Wild*, which makes the connection between the battle of the sexes and the battle for the environment; that is, the connection between feminism and ecology. There Collard argues the transition from matriarchy to patriarchy as occurring alongside the transition from a gathering culture to a hunting culture. The emergence of the hunt, for Collard, signifies man's rape of the earth and of women and the alienation of man from nature and women. This eventually led to warfare, the destruction of the animal kingdom extended to human beings. In religious worship this transition was manifested in the replacement of the worship of the female goddess by worship of the male god.[14]

Lending credence to this, Amadiume relates the case of the domestication and sub-ordination of the Igbo goddess, Idemili (river goddess) through marriage to the lesser hunter/deity, Aho, as indicating the imposition of patriarchy on an originally matriarchal Igbo society.[15]

Sulemane Cisse's film, *Ye'elen* also serves to highlight the parallels between the battle of the sexes and man's destruction and domination of nature. The film mainly revolves around four characters: a young Bambara man named Nianankoro, his mother, his father and his wife; although it centres mainly on the struggle for power between father and son. Nianankoro's mother apparently hands down to her son powers which she has in the form of a pyramidal jewel (eye of Kore). This could be interpreted as a matrilineal act. The father has powers but abuses these in a bid to destroy his son. The film does not go into the dynamics of the relationships between the men and women in much depth, but appears to be, on one level, a struggle (for reasons which are not clear) between the mother (through the son) and the father representing, respectively, good and evil. Before going off to a final battle with his father Nianankoro hands his agbada (shawl) to his wife, instructing her that it must be given to the child she is soon to conceive when the child has grown old enough. In the end there is a showdown between Nianankoro and his father which results in their destruction as well as the destruction of the environment. In the duel their powers are represented by two totemic objects, each studded with a pyramidal jewel – 'eye of Kore' – apparently a source of magical power. This closing scene is strongly suggestive of a nuclear explosion and the destruction of the earth as a result of man's abuse of science. After the destruction it is the woman, wife of Nianankoro who picks up the pieces, gathering the magic wing and eye of Kore from where Nianankoro had placed it to do battle. The child, now grown, unearths one of two ostrich eggs (possibly signifying the choice between good and evil) buried in the desert sand and gives it to the mother who replaces it. She then places the agbada, a symbol of the boy's patrilineal inheritance from his father, Nianankoro, over his body and hands down to him the 'wing of Kore', the totemic object with which his father waged battle. The desert, it would seem, symbolises the barrenness after the destruction wrought by man. The male child's removal of the egg and its replacement by the mother appears to say to us that it is the woman who restores order after the men have wrought chaos. But then the camera focuses on the shifting slopes of the desert sand signifying, perhaps, the instability of the situation and that it would not be long before the male child grew up and man once again abused his powers for evil and destruction.

Ifi Amadiume refers to this cycle through the Ohaffia saying 'father's penis scatters, mother's womb gathers', referring to woman's role as gathering and restoring order after the chaos brought about by man's irresponsibility.[16]

INDIVIDUALISM

The opposition of Western culture to the culture of Africans and other peoples of the South has become largely the opposition of the philosophies of spiritual and material individualism to spiritual and material collectivism. As Gablik observes:

> In traditional societies, the individual lives submerged in tradition which is, for him, immutable reality, transmitted from a venerable past; the individual does nothing on his own account, apart from the social group. Indeed, nothing is more terrible than to be cast out of the collective and to remain alone. It is hard for us to realise that modern western notions of the individual – his selfhood, his rights and his freedom – have no meaning in the Orient or for primitive man.[17]

The material individualism of Western society is the philosophy that each individual should be left alone to struggle for his/her own good. It promotes the idea of the independence of the individual whereby whatever property belongs to the individual belongs to him or her exclusively; it does not follow that it also belongs to his or her family (certainly not any relations beyond the immediate family). This is one aspect of the break-up of the family in Western society which also threatens to do the same in the urban parts of the African and Southern world where the influence of European culture is inevitable.

In contrast to this, African people traditionally practice collectivism through the concept of the extended family. The individual is not conceived as independent (materially or emotionally) of the community or the environment. In regard to property, what a person has belongs to the family.

This idea of dependence and hence an inseparable link between the individual, the community and the environment is a form of collectivism Africans share with other peoples of the

Southern world. It is beautifully emphasized by these words of Duwamish (native American) chief Seattle:

> All things are connected. Whatever befalls the earth befalls the sons of the earth.... If men spit on the ground they spit upon themselves .... Man did not weave the web of life; he is merely a strand in it. Whatever he does to the web he does to himself.[18]

Even more concisely, there is an African proverb which effectively says: *Don't pee in the river you have to drink from.*

The spiritual individualism of the West derives from Christianity, which traditionally emphasizes a vertical relationship between the individual and God, where moral or immoral action has no consequence outside the sphere of the individual. It is the individual alone who is punished with eternal suffering or rewarded with eternal paradise. Russel cites the emphasis on the soul in Christianity as leading to individualism.[19] This is not surprising; for once the consequences of individual action are restricted to the individual, self-salvation will become each person's priority. This is opposite to the view in African society. What the individual does has consequences for the community in this life as is evinced by the Igbo proverb, 'If one finger brought oil, it soiled all the others'.[20]

ESTRANGEMENT OF ETHICS AND MORALITY FROM THE DEVELOPMENT AND APPLICATION OF KNOWLEDGE

Perhaps the strongest theme occurring in the section on *Ethics and Moral Experience* concerned the corporate or collective nature of moral responsibility in African philosophy. This, we recall, together with the idea of a community which includes the ancestors, the living and the unborn, implies an ecologically orientated ethics in which our concern for those who come after us is reflected in the state in which we choose to leave our social and natural environment. But today the new born enter a world with polluted air and waters, a world with rapidly diminishing plant and animal life, a world where millions starve whilst food is plentiful, a world where regimes propped up by western financial institutions and supported by a greedy indigenous elite deny basic human rights.

Human knowledge (particularly Western science and technology) has been abused to dominate nature (including human beings) as opposed to maintaining the ecological balance. This unethical application of knowledge reveals that no connection is made by science with ethics and ecology. The tendency to compartmentalize or isolate these issues instead of seeing them as interrelated is reflected in such hideous household sayings as: 'art and politics don't mix', 'religion and politics don't mix', 'sport and politics don't mix'.

Western scientific research, we have noted, is short-sighted in that the long-term effects of research products for the environment and for future generations are never investigated. Today we are seeing the long term consequences of a science which is not guided by these considerations.

Hountondji, we may recall, despite all else, urges Africans to take the opposite of the European path. In so doing he has succinctly pointed out the direction in which our art, science and ethics need to develop as a world system. Our task here has been to contribute to the laying of a foundation for this development, greatly advanced by the work of such African thinkers as those whose names have been mentioned in these pages.

TOWARDS A HOLISTIC SYSTEM OF EDUCATION

What practical significance can all of this have for Africans at home and abroad? On the continent and in the diaspora we have inherited colonial systems of education which are Eurocentric. Such systems serve only to alienate future generations of African women and men from their Africanness, cultivating the lob-sided and anti-holistic worldview of the European world. As Cisse's film, *Ye'elen*, seems to warn us, we urgently need to avoid cultivating in ourselves the attitude whereby knowledge is abused as a means of dominating and destroying people and environment for the sake of power and short-term material gains. On the continent and in the diaspora we need to devise a system of education appropriate to our present day needs and which presents as united those things which the anti-holistic worldview has divided. Specifically, we must emphasize the co-existence of art and science, reason and emotion, woman and man. In this way we would encourage the development of wholesome and therefore healthy minded individuals. Africans abroad could establish and run supplementary schools based on the same principles. The operation of such systems on the continent and in the diaspora depend on the political will to put them into practice. In many cases this is lacking. Supplementary schools abroad could therefore provide models which could be adapted to the continent and the diaspora.

In bringing together science, art and ethics the functional side of art would be explored as in the use of mythological forms in conjunction with plain explanations to relate scientific ideas and ethical principles. Such a mode of explanation would much more likely captivate and interest the child, leaving a stronger impression than if the facts are conveyed in an academic and uninteresting way.

The education system should be such that the children are taught that the natural line of descent is through the mother. This can be demonstrated as beyond doubt once it is understood that all human beings are conceived by woman.

Also, the children should be made aware that the traits of both sexes exist within each human being. Within every man there is a woman and within every woman, a man. Therefore any man who hates women is a man who hates an aspect of himself which he cannot come to terms with. His hatred for women is therefore an externalization of this self-hatred. The Dogon of Mali and indeed most African societies believe that a child's sex is undecided until puberty. Thus the symbolic meaning of circumcision is to take away something female from the male (that is, the male 'vagina', the foreskin) and something male from the female (that is, the female 'penis', the clitoris). We do not have to agree with female circumcision to understand the logical consistency of the act. We must draw a distinction here between the symbolic meaning and the symbolic act. The way in which we enact this symbolism need not be indispensable simply because it is tradition. We need to be self-critical and discerning enough to do away with traditions or aspects of traditions that are harmful. This does not, however, mean that the symbolism is not valid and that it cannot be enacted in some other less harmful way.

The male/female nature of each human being is also portrayed through the manner in which the ancient African gods of Egypt occurred in male/female pairs. These issues in regard to man and woman should be brought to children's attention early on so that respect for the opposite sex is inculcated into the male child.

Lastly, many would be keen to know what would happen in regard to the study of religion and philosophy. The important point to note here is that African religion is not traditionally an institutionalized religion. It would appear that in most of Africa the word for religion (and the same could be said for art) does not exist, revealing that religion (like art) is so much interwoven into the fabric of daily life that it cannot be isolated into its own little corner or placed within four walls on one day a week whilst remaining absent from the life of the individual for the rest of the week.

Though this would probably form the topic of another book, it is this author's belief that African religion up until the coming of colonialism had not moved backwards or remained static since the times of ancient Egypt, but had actually developed to the state of being totally de-institutionalised. In other words, de-institutionalization is held here to be the mark of a highly developed religion (and, again, precisely the same can be said of African art).

Attention has been drawn to the parallels between African religion and African art, indeed, all religion and art. This parallel between art and religion is a key to the clarification of the essential natures of art and religion. Religion is like art in that each person has his/her own unique way of seeing it or living it.

African religious study should have a special place in any African educational curriculum in the sense that its philosophy should create an attitude permeating the study of all other subjects. But it is also absolutely imperative that the curriculum includes the study of comparative religion, in a manner which will inevitably be Afrocentric. This would ensure that narrow and intolerant religious attitudes are not developed whilst at the same time ensuring a grounding in one's own culture. Comparative religion would also be vital in enabling students to see religion in perspective as something that should not be dissociated from its cultural or historical context. It would be of immense benefit for students to see the fundamental aspects that world religions have in common, quite a few of which have been outlined in this work. It would be important for students to appreciate that the cultures of the world and hence the religions of the world have not developed in isolation and in a sporadic manner, but in one involving the historical development of one from another as well as the interaction of cultures. It is unlikely that human civilization had more than a single source. For this reason it is not surprising to discover all of the worlds' major religions as having fundamental aspects in common. Such an approach to the study of religion would be a safeguard against religion becoming institutionalised (that is, fixed and static) rather than being a practical guide and an adaptable philosophy to the life we live in the present.

In regard to the calls from some quarters for the resuscitation of an African faith the logic is the same. In many cases the wish to resuscitate an African faith is the wish to see it institutionalized in the same way that Euro-christianity is. The philosophy of African religion must be made widely available to the people for them to take whatever can benefit them from it, rather than become an institution which eventually ends up imposing itself in a bid to gain converts. African religion and philosophy, which is holistic, optimistic and life-affirming must by its nature be lived in order to thrive, through our art, science, ethics and morality. It should in spirit permeate our daily lives. Our prayers should not be found imprisoned within four walls, but in the diligence with which we work, create and live.

This holistic outlook on knowledge and the notion of collective or corporate moral responsibility shared by Africans with other peoples of the South offers the world an alternative to the Euro-centrism which presently threatens the existence of humankind. The idea of the continuity of past, present and future in African and other Southern and Eastern philosophies lays down the moral duty of the present generation: to pave the way for unborn generations.

NOTES

PREFACE

1. This accords with Cheikh Anta Diop's theory in *Cultural Unity of Black Africa* that Northern cultures were traditionally patriarchal and Southern ones, matriarchal.

INTRODUCTION

1. L.S.B. Leakey, '*The Evolution of Man on the African Continent*'; Tarikh Vol. I, No. 3: *Man in Africa*, Longman, 1966, p.7-11.
2. See his *African Origin of Civilization: Myth or Reality*, Lawrence Hill and Co. (USA), 1974 edition.
3. Ibid., p.1.
4. Martin Bernal, *Black Athena*, Vol. I: *The Fabrication of Ancient Greece*, Free Association Books, London, 1987, p.241.
5. E.A. Wallis Budge, *The Egyptian Book of the Dead*, Dover, N.Y., 1967 edition, p.xi.
6. J.S. Mbiti, *African Religions and Philosophy*, Heinemann, 1969.
7. E.G. Parrinder, *African Traditional Religion*, 1974, third edition, p.19.
8. C.A. Diop, *Cultural Unity of Black Africa*, Karnak House, 1989 edition.
9. See his introduction to P. Hountondji's *African Philosophy: Myth or Reality*, Hutchinson University Library for Africa, London, Melbourne, Sydney, Auckland, Johannesburg, 1983.
10. E.A. Wallis Budge, *The Egyptian Book of the Dead*, 1967 edit., p.xi (brackets are mine).
11. B. Reed, *Rebel in the Soul*, 1978, Wildwood House, London; Bookwax, Australia, p.11.
12. E.A. Wallis Budge, *Egyptian Book of the Dead*, 1967 edit., p.xcviii.
13. (i) M. Karenga, *The Husia*, Kawaida Publications, Los Angeles, 1984, pp.91–98.
    (ii) J. Breasted, *The Dawn of Conscience*, N.Y., 1934, p.xv.
14. F.A. Yates, *Giordano Bruno and the Hermetic Tradition*, RKP, 1964, p.23.

15. E.A. Wallis Budge, *Egyptian Book of the Dead*, 1967 edit., p.xciii.
16. J.S. Mbiti, *Introduction to African Religion*, 1975, p.36.
17. J.S. Mbiti, *African Religions and Philosophy*, 1969, p.205.
18. Ibid., p.210.
19. Ibid., pp.205–206.
20. Y. ben-Jochannan, *Black Man of the Nile & his Family*, Alkebulan Books, N.Y., 1981, , p.191.
21. M. Bernal, op.cit., pp.109–112.
22. Marcus Garvey quoted from Tony Martin's *Race First*, Greenwood Press, Mass., 1976, p.84.
23. Ibid., p.87.
24. Dr. Y. ben-Jochannan, op.cit., p.460.
25. M. Griaule, *Conversations with Ogotemmeli*, Oxford University, 1955, pp.xiii–xvi.
26. R.A. Schwaller de Lubicz, *Symbol and the Symbolic*, Inner Traditions International, 1949.
27. B. Reed, *Rebel in the Soul*, 1978.
28. Mbiti in *African Religions & Philosophy* (1969) says (p.33) that African belief is not pantheistic since there is no evidence 'that people consider God to be everything and everything to be God'. But in the same chapter he provides evidence, as he does elsewhere, that God is generally believed to occupy all space and all time. Given the fact that Africans identify space with objects and time with events, as he also explains in the same work, it is definitely implied that God is everything and that everything is God.
29. K. Nkrumah, *Consciencism*, Panaf, London 1964, pp.78–106. Also see P. Tempels, *Bantu Philosophy*, Paris, 1959 and J. Jahn, *Muntu*, 1961.
30. D. Bohm, *The Special Theory of Relativity*, New York, 1965, p.116.
31. K. Nkrumah, op. cit., p.101.
32. Y. ben-Jochannan, op.cit., p.478.
33. J.S. Mbiti, op.cit., p.229.
34. A. Cabral, *Return to the Source: Selected Speeches*, Monthly Review Press, London & N.Y., 1973, p.40.
35. Uthman 'Amr Ibn Bahr Al-Jahiz, *The Glory of the Black Race*, L.A., p.50.
36. G. Parrinder, *The World's Living Religions*, Pan, London, 1964, pp.14–15.
37. C.A. Diop, *African Origin of Civilization*, Lawrence Hill & Co., Westport, 1974, p.123.
38. Ibid., p.124.

39. George Bankes, *African Carvings*, Ditchling Press, Sussex, 1975, p.10.
40. P.J. Houndtondji, *African Philosophy: Myth or Reality*, 1983, p.54.
41. Ibid., pp.128–9.
42. K. Popper, *Conjectures and Refutations*, RKP, 1963, p.17.
43. J.S. Mbiti, op.cit., p.57.
44. H.H. Adams III, *'African Observers of the Universe'* in Van Sertima, ed., *Blacks in Science: Ancient & Modern*, Journal of African Civilizations, New Jersey, 1985, p.31.
45. Ibid., p.32.

Part I

INTRODUCTION

1. A secret body of knowledge confined to chosen initiates of proven wisdom; for they were not to misuse the power it would give them. The goal of the system was the enlightenment or 'deification' of man. This was achieved in three stages:
   (a.) The Mortals: Students on probation and under instruction. They had not yet achieved experience in the 'Inner Vision'. (*Initiation.*)
   (b.) The Intelligences: Students had attained the 'Inner Vision' and had received 'Mind' or 'Nous'. (*Divine Inspiration/illumination.*)
   (c.) The Creators of Light: Students had achieved oneness with the 'Spiritual Consciousness'. (*Perfection/enlightenment/deification.*)
2. Heraclitus thought the fundamental element was fire; Thales thought it was water; Anaximander thought there were three: earth, fire and water.
3. B. Russell, *History of Western Philosophy*, London 1961 ed., p.25.
4. Ibid., p.45.
5. British Museum.
6. From one of the last lectures given by Dr. C.A. Diop at the Camden Centre, London, Conference on *Afrikan Origin of Civilization*, 12th January 1985, presented by Karnak House.
7. M. Griaule & G. Dieterlen, 'The Dogon' in D. Forde, ed., *African Worlds*, Oxford, 1954, p.85.
8. M. Griaule, *Conversations with Ogotemmeli*, Oxford, 1965, p.24.

9. E.A. Wallis Budge, *The Egyptian Book of the Dead*, Dover, N.Y., 1967 edition, p.xcix. The brackets are mine.
10. E.A. Wallis Budge, *The Gods of the Egyptians*, Dover, N.Y., 1904, p.283.
11. Ibid., p.285.
12. Ibid.
13. Ibid., p.287.
14. No logical difficulty lies in attributing existence to nothingness (see B. Russell, *History of Western Philosophy*, p.88); for to say that nothing (no thing) exists is not the same as to say nothingness, an essence or quality, exists.
15. M.D. Vernon, *Psychology of Perception*, 1962, p.32.
16. J.P. Sartre, *Being and Nothingness*, 1943, pp.9–11. See his example illustrating this.
17. B. Davidson, *The Africans*, Longman, Harlow & London, 1969, p.173.
18. As a further example of the oneness of traditional African and ancient Egyptian religion we note the Egyptians possessed the gods Nut and Seb who were gods of the sky and the earth. Nut was the female principle of the primeval void or water. Nu, and Seb, god of the earth, was her husband. In this, through the union of male and female principles, we see the concrete as opposed to abstract representation of the doctrine of opposites.
19. B. Davidson, op.cit., p.173.
20. M. Griaule, op.cit., pp.16–23.
21. P. Mercier, '*The Fon of Dahomey*' in D. Forde, ed., *African Worlds*, Oxford 1954, p.21.
22. G. Liendhart, '*The Shilluk of the Upper Nile*', Ibid., p.155.
23. B. Davidson, op.cit., p.173.
24. P. Mercier, op.cit., p.217.
25. Bohm speaks of how new born infants acquire their concepts of space, time, permanence of substance, etc., which, in the form he describes them, are Ideas. D. Bohm, *The Special Theory of Relativity*, N.Y., 1965, pp.187–196.
26. The observation of this paradox originates from Kant, op.cit., p.403.
27. In speaking of attempts to make sense of the world about us, the reference is made specifically to scientific investigation.
28. E.A. Wallis Budge, *The Egyptian Book of the Dead*, 1967 ed., N.Y., p.251.
29. Ibid., p.168.
30. Ibid., p.44.
31. Ibid., Introduction, p.lxxiv.
32. In further establishing the link between traditional and ancient

African religion and philosophy, we note that this conception of God as a potter is prevalent on the continent today (See J. Mbiti, *African Religions and Philosophy* and G. Parrinder, *African Traditional Religion*.)

33. Champollion-Figeac, *Egypte*, Paris 1839, p.245.
34. E.A. Wallis Budge, *Egyptian Book of the Dead*, 1967 ed., N.Y., p.xi.
35. See C.A. Diop, *African Origin of Civilization*, p.6 and C. Williams, *Destruction of Black Civilizations*, p.116.
36. E.A. Wallis Budge, op.cit., p.xcii.
37. Ibid., p.cxxvii.
38. Ibid., p.249.
39. Ibid., p.251.
40. P. Tempels, *Bantu Philosophy*, 1959, pp.50–51.
41. Newell S. Booth, '*God and the Gods in West Africa*' in *African Religions*, Newell S. Booth, ed., Nok Publishers International, N.Y., London, Lagos, 1977, p.177.
42. Newell Booth, op.cit., p.177.
43. O. Imasogie, *African Traditional Religions*, Ibadan University, 1985, p.26.
44. *A Dictionary of Philosophy*, Editorial consultant, A. Flew, Pan Books, 1979, p.14.
45. Ibid., p.261.
46. K. Nkrumah, *Consciencism*, Panaf, London, 1964, p.84.
47. L. Barrett, '*African Religion in the Americas*' in Newell S. Booth, ed., *African Religions*, Nok Publications International, London, Lagos, N.Y., 1977, p.185.
48. From papyrus No. 10188, British Museum. Translation in *Archaelogia*, Vol. lii, pp.440–443.
49. E.A. Wallis Budge, op.cit., p.xcviii.
50. Ibid., p.251.
51. Ibid.
52. Ibid., p.xcii.
53. Ibid., p.326.

CHAPTER ONE

1. J.S. Mbiti, *Introduction to African Religion*, 1975, pp.32–33.
2. This scene is a common depiction in Egyptian tombs and papyri.
3. Various versions of this account are given in Chapter II, Part Two. See also E.A. Wallis Budge, *Egyptian Book of the Dead*, p.xciii–c.

4. C.A. Diop, *African Origin of Civilization*, p.102.
5. J.S. Mbiti, op.cit., p.77.
6. W. Nobles, 'Ancient African Thought and the Development of African Psychology' in M. Karenga, J.H. Carruthers, eds., *Kemet and the African Worldview*, 1986, p.103.
7. M. Griaule, *Conversations with Ogotemmeli*, Oxford 1965, p.xiv–xvi.
8. By 'essential attributes' it is meant that they are what make phenomena phenomena. In the same way there are certain things which make a book a book. A book has leaves which contain writing and it exists to be read. These three different aspects of a book might be called its essential attributes, because if it did not have at least the first of these we could not call it a book. The *essential attributes* of something then, are the properties that a thing has which make it what it is.
9. Obviously the void has no actual experienceable attributes, but it is perfectly sensible, for instance, to think of nothingness as a non-entity, and this may be said to be a concept which belongs essentially to it. Similarly, infinity and continuity are concepts which can be thought of as belonging essentially to the void; in this sense infinity, continuity and non-entity are its *conceptual attributes*.
10. J.S. Mbiti, op.cit., p.35.
11. Ibid. and E.A. Wallis Budge.
12. A. Churchward, *Signs and Symbols of Primordial Man*, Westport, Conn., Greenwood Press, 1978, p.204.
13. Knowing that something is true does not only consist in seeing that it is true rationally; it also consists in *feeling* and *believing* that it is true. Often our reason has to be ratified by our feeling. If this is not the case, we tend to retrace the path of our reasoning again in order to erase lingering doubt. Conversely, we can *feel* that we know something to be a truth before we have demonstrated it to ourselves rationally.

CHAPTER TWO

1. This is a paradox of motion devised from the sort of argument used by Zeno of Elea. See any dictionary of philosophy for *Zeno's Paradoxes* (e.g., *A Dictionary of Philosophy*, Editorial Consultant, A. Flew, Pan Books, London, 1979).
2. J. Pappademos '*An Outline of Africa's Role in the History of Physics*', in I. Van Sertima, editor, *Blacks in Science: Ancient*

      and Modern, Transaction Books, London & New Brunswick (USA), 1985, p.184.
3. Ibid., p.184.
4. M. Bernal, *Black Athena*, Vol.I, London 1987, p.197.
5. Ibid., p.295.
6. Ibid., p.106.
7. R. Rucker, *Infinity and the Mind*, Paladin Books, London, 1984, p.64.
8. M. Kac, S. Ulam, *Mathematics & Logic*, Penguin, Middlesex., 1979, pp.23–25.
9. R. Rucker, op.cit., p.43.
10. Bertrand Russel, *History of Western Philosophy*, Unwin, London, 1976, (first published 1946), pp.783–784.
11. Ibid., p.46.
12. J.S. Mbiti, *Introduction to African Religions*, 1975, p.36.
13. In parallel, the Ideas of Absolute Good, Absolute Moral Law and Unfailing Will, which we shall meet ahead, are embodied by its ethical significance.
14. W. Kaufman, *Cosmic Frontiers of Relativity*, Penguin, 1979, pp.66–68.
15. It is not valid for very large and very small spatio-temporal (space-time) domains, respectively, of the order of the size of the known universe and of sizes much smaller than sub-atomic particles. See D. Bohm, *Special Theory of Relativity*, W.A. Benjamin Inc., N.Y., Amsterdam, 1965, p.109.
16. K. Popper, *Conjectures and Refutations*, RKP, London & Henley, 1963.
17. J.S. Mbiti, *African Religions & Philosophy*, 1969, p.27.
18. How this is done, we shall see in Part Two.
19. G.G.M. James, *Stolen Legacy*, 1954, p.147.
20. A. Beiser, *Concepts of Modern Physics*, 1963, p.441.
21. B. Davidson, *The Africans*, Longman, Harlow & London, 1969, pp.173–4.
22. E.A. Wallis Budge, *The Egyptian Book of the Dead*, Chapter LXXXIV.
23. J.S. Mbiti, *Introduction to African Religions*, 1975, p.118.
24. J.S. Mbiti, *African Religions & Philosophy*, 1969, p.160.
25. E.A. Wallis Budge, op.cit., pp.lviii–lxx.
26. I. Kant, *Critique of Pure Reason*, 1934 ed., p.94.
27. M.D. Vernon, *Psychology of Perception*, 1962, p.32.
28. I. Kant, op.cit., pp.240–249.
29. To briefly deal with a point of interest arising from this we might note that not everything located in space is available to the senses. Even though there are physical entities which are

invisible or inaudible due to our not having the technology to detect them (e.g., possibly certain frequencies of radiation), they still possess, even now, the possibility of being experienced by the senses, even if aided.

30. J.S. Mbiti, op.cit., p.161.
    J.H. Carruthers, *Essays in Ancient Egyptian Studies*, Timbuctu Publishers, Los Angeles, 1984, pp.65–66.
31. J.S. Mbiti, ibid., p.161.
32. G.G.M. James, op.cit., p.27.
    See also, B. Reed, *Rebel in the Soul*, 1978, pp.108,110.
33. J.S. Mbiti, op.cit., p.29.
34. St. Elmo Numan, *Dictionary of Asian Philosophies*, London 1979, pp.20–21.
35. J.S. Mbiti, ibid., pp.25–26.
36. E.A. Wallis Budge, *Egyptian Religion*, RKP, 1979, p.166.
37. I. Kant, op.cit., pp.346–358.

CHAPTER THREE

1. George Thompson, *The Human Essence – The Sources of Science and Art*, China Policy Study Group, London, 1974, p.88.
2. Ibid., p.88.
3. Peter Tompkins, *Secrets of the Great Pyramid*, Allen Lane, 1973, p.103.
4. Ibid., p.48.
5. Ibid., p.75.
6. Ibid., pp.92, 113.
7. Beatrice Lumpkin, '*The Pyramids: Ancient Showcase of African Science and Technology*', in I. Van Sertima, ed., *Blacks in Science*, Transaction Books, 1985, p.71.
8. P. Tompkins, op.cit., p.194.
9. A non-algebraic number. It is a number which cannot be written down in a finite number of digits and can only be represented geometrically. It cannot be placed in an orderly sequence. Diop alludes to the Egyptian representation of a transcendental number in his lecture. *The Antiquity of Afrikan Civilization* at the Camden Centre, London. First Annual Conference of the *Afrikan Origin of Civilization*, 12th January, 1985, under the auspices of Karnak House.
10. H.H. Adams III, '*African Observers of the Universe: The Sirius Question*', in I. Van Sertima, ed., *Blacks in Science*, 1985, pp.31–32.
11. J.G. Frazer, *The Golden Bough*, Macmillan, London, 1983 (abridged), p.932.

12. Ibid., p.14.
13. A. Einstein & L. Infield, *The Evolution of Physics*, Cambridge University Press, 1971, p.6.
14. Dr. C. Finch, '*African Background of Medical Science*', in Van Sertina, op. cit., p.14.
15. J. Jahn, *Muntu*, Faber and Faber, London, 1961, pp.127–132.
16. Ibid., pp.127–128.
17. Ibid., p.128.
18. Ibid.
19. Ibid.
20. D. Bohm, *The Special Theory of Relativity*, New York, 1965, p.49.
21. J.S. Mbiti, *African Religions and Philosophy*, 1969, p.27.
22. K. Nkrumah, *Consciencism*, 1964, p.97.
23. D. Bohm, *The Special Theory of Relativity*, N.Y., 1965, p.116.
24. P. Tempels, *Bantu Philosophy*, Presence Africaine, Paris, 1959, pp.50–1.
25. M. Bernal, *Black Athena*, London, 1987, p.175.
26. K. Nkrumah, op.cit., p.82.
27. L. Barrett, '*African Religion in the Americas*', in Newell S. Booth, ed., *African Religions*, Nok Publications International, London, Lagos, N.Y., 1977, p.185.
28. L. Segy, *African Sculpture*, Dover, N.Y., 1958, p.2.
29. R. Sieber, '*Some Aspects of Religion and Art in Africa*', in Newell S. Booth, ed., op.cit., p.149.
30. Ibid., p.145.
31. J. Mbiti, *Introduction to African Religions*, London, 1975, p.22.
32. P.S. Wingert, *Primitive Art*, N.Y., 1962, p.65.
33. L. Segy, *Masks of Black Africa*, Dover, N.Y., 1976, p.12.
34. R. Sieber, op.cit., p.147.
35. P.S. Wingert, op.cit., p.43.
36. L. Segy, op.cit., p.12.
37. See P.S. Wingert, op.cit.
38. Ibid., p.37.
39. R. Sieber, op.cit., p.146.
40. Ibid.
41. P.S. Wingert, op.cit., p.44.
42. L. Segy, op.cit., p.39. See also his book, *African Sculpture*, Dover. N.Y., 1958, pp.18–19.
43. L. Segy, *Masks of Black Africa*, p.40.
44. P.S. Wingert, op.cit., pp.38–40.
45. L. Segy, op.cit., p.40.
46. C. Zaslavsky, *Africa Counts*, Prindle, Weber & Schmidt, Boston, 1973, pp.173–174.
47. J. Jahn, op.cit., p.188.

48. J.H. Kwabena Nketia, *The Music of Africa*, Victor Gollancz, London, 1975, p.184.
49. O. Walton, *Music: Black, White & Blue*, William Morrow & Co. Inc, New York, 1972, p.13.

Part II

INTRODUCTION

1. M. Griaule & G. Dieterlein, '*The Dogon*' in D. Forde, ed., *African Worlds*, Oxford, 1954, p.87.
2. D. Bohm, *Special Theory of Relativity*, 1965, p.187.

CHAPTER ONE

1. J. Piaget, *The Origin of Intelligence in the Child*, RKP 1953, p.128.
2. D. Bohm, *The Special Theory of Relativity*, 1965, p.187.
3. Ibid., p.191.
4. G. Frege, *Foundations of Arithmetic*, Blackwell, Oxford, 1980, pp.39–44.
5. J.S. Mbiti, *African Religions & Philosophy*, 1969, p.214.
6. L. Segy, *Masks of Black Africa*, Dover, N.Y. 1976, p.12.
7. E.A. Wallis Budge, *The Gods of the Egyptians*, Dover, N.Y., 1904, p.415.
8. I. Kant, *Critique of Pure Reason*, 1934 translation, pp.94–95.
9. G. Frege, op.cit., pp.27–33.
10. D. Bohm, *The Special Theory of Relativity*, N.Y., 1965, pp.190–2.

CHAPTER TWO

1. M. Griaule & G. Dieterlen, '*The Dogon*' in D. Forde, ed., *African Worlds*, 1954.
2. We are reminded here of the seven fundamental wavelengths of vibration of light (that is, the seven colours of the spectrum).
3. B. Davidson, *The Africans*, 1969, pp.172–173.
4. E. A. Wallis Budge, *Egyptian Religion*, RKP 1979 ed., pp.22–23.
5. E.A. Wallis Budge, *The Egyptian Book of the Dead*, pp.xcix–c.
6. A language spoken in Senegal, West Africa.
7. C.A. Diop, *African Origin of Civilization*, 1974, p.109.
8. G.G.M. James, *Stolen Legacy*, 1954, p.64.

9. J.H. Carruthers, *Essays in Ancient Egyptian Studies*, 1984, p.57.
10. J.S. Mbiti, *African Religions and Philosophy*, 1969, p.19.
11. Ibid., p.27.
12. Ibid., p.17.
13. A. Grunbaum, *The Philosophical Problems of Space and Time*, RKP, 1964 (reference to his discussion on measurement where he notes that size is not an inherent property of an object, but one relative to external objects), pp.44–48.
14. It is interesting to compare the supreme God of the Dogon, *Amma*, with the one God of the ancient Egyptians, *Ammon*. In addition to this, the Dogon god Nummo, which often formed a duo with Amma, is representative of a primeval water spirit. We note that the primeval water of the Egyptians was Nu. The names and ideas are so similar as to imply the direct descendence of Dogon religion from ancient Egypt.
15. M. Griaule, *Conversations with Ogotommeli*, Oxford, 1965, pp.16–17.
16. C. Diop, *African Origin of Civilization*, Lawrence Hill & Co., 1974, p.109.
17. It seems curious that we should be able to give a definition to such a supreme abstraction; but this is only because we have defined void in terms of its opposite, matter. The void in itself cannot be defined. In similar ways, the infinite can only be defined in terms of the finite numbers, and God can only be conceived in the image of a human being. The primeval void, therefore, also qualifies as an Idea.
18. *Egyptian Book of the Dead*, Chapter lxxiv, plate xxviii.
19. E.A. Wallis-Budge, *The Gods of the Egyptiaans: Vol. 2*, Dover, N.Y., 1969, p. 299.
20. E.I. Metuh, *God and Man in African Religion*, Geoffrey Chapman, London, 1981, p. 68.
21. Ibid., p. 88.

APPENDIX

1. T. Obenga, '*African Philosophy of the Pharaonic Period*' in I. Van Sertima, ed., *Egypt Revisited*, (Journal of African Civilizations), 1989, p.317.
2. Ibid., p.304.
3. E.A. Wallis Budge, *Egyptian Religion*, RKP, 1979, pp.23-24.
4. E.A. Wallis Budge, *Egyptian Book of the Dead*, Dover, 1967, p.251.

5. Ibid., p.338.
6. Ibid., p.340.
7. T. Obenga, '*African Philosophy of the Pharaonic Period*' in I. Van Sertima, ed., *Egypt Revisited*, (Journal of African Civilizations), 1989, p.297.
8. Ibid., p.304.
9. E.A. Wallis Budge, *Egyptian Religion*, RKP, 1979, p.25.

Part III

CHAPTER ONE

1. G.G.M. James, *Stolen Legacy*, 1954, p.73.
2. Ibid.
3. E.A. Wallis Budge, *Egyptian Book of the Dead*, p.lxxviii.
4. J.S. Mbiti, *Introduction to African Religions*, 1975, p.204.
5. K. Nkrumah, *Consciencism*, 1964, p.93.
6. J.S. Mbiti, *African Religions and Philosophy*, 1969, p.214.

CHAPTER TWO

1. F. Fanon, *Black Skin, White Masks*, 1967, pp.216–217.
2. Ibid., p.217.
3. Ibid., p.89.
4. Ibid.
5. L. Adele Jinadu, *Fanon: In Search of the African Revolution*, Fourth Dimension Publishers, Nigeria, 1980, pp.143–8.
6. J.S. Mbiti, *African Religions and Philosophy*, 1969, p.133.
7. M. Karenga, *The Husia*, p.32.
8. R.D. Abrahams, *African Folktales*, Pantheon Books, N.Y., 1983, pp.42–5.
9. K. Nkrumah, *Consciencism*, 1964, p.97.
10. G.G.M. James, *Stolen Legacy*, 1954, pp.30–31.
11. Ibid., p.73.
12. Ibid., p.27.
13. Ibid.
14. J.S. Mbiti, op.cit., p.164.
    D. M'Timkulu '*Some Aspects of Zulu Religion*' in N.S. Booth, ed., *African Religions*, Nok Publishers, N.Y. 1977, p.19.
15. L. Segy, *Masks of Black Africa*, Dover, N.Y., 1976, p.12.

AFTERWORD

1. Chancellor Williams, *The Destruction of Black Civilizations*, 1976, p.123.
2. G.G.M. James, *Stolen Legacy*, 1954, p.154.
3. Y. Ben-Jochannan, *Black Man of the Nile and his Family*, 1981 ed., p.202.
4. C. Williams, op.cit., pp.83–91.
5. Amilcar Cabral, *Return to the Source*, Selected Speeches, 1973, p.43.
6. Kwame Nkrumah, *Consciencism*, 1964, p.79.
7. C.A. Diop, *Cultural Unity of Black Africa*, 1978, p.12.
8. I. Okpewho, *Myth in Africa*, Cambridge University Press, 1983, p.222.
9. M. Bernal, *Black Athena*, p.241.
10. E.A. Wallis Budge, *Gods of the Egyptians*, Vol.1, p.143.
11. B. Russel, *History of Western Philosophy*, Unwin, 1979, p.189.
12. C.A. Diop, op.cit., pp.68–70.
13. I. Amadiume, *Afrikan Matriarchal Foundations: The Igbo Case*, Karnak House, 1987.
14. A. Collard, J. Contrucci, *Rape of the Wild*, Women's Press, 1987, p.61.
15. I. Amadiume, op.cit., p.61.
16. Ibid., p.19.
17. S. Gablik, *Has Modernism Failed?*, Thames & Hudson, 1984, p.30.
18. A. Collard, J. Contrucci, op.cit., p.24.
19. B. Russel, *Why I am not a Christian*, Unwin Paperbacks, 1979, p.34.
20. C. Achebe, *Things Fall Apart*, Heinemann, 1958, p.87.

BIBLIOGRAPHY

Abrahams, R.D., *African Folktales*, Pantheon Books, N.Y., 1983.
Achebe, C., *Things Fall Apart*, Heinemann, London, 1958.
Al-Jahiz, U., *Book of the Glory of the Black Race*, W. Preston, L.A., 1981.
Amadiume, I., *Afrikan Matriarchal Foundations: The Igbo Case*, Karnak House, London, 1987.
Bankes, G., *African Carvings*, Ditchling Press, Sussex, 1975.
Beiser, A., *Concepts of Modern Physics*, McGraw-Hill, N.Y., 1963.
Ben-Jochannan, Y., *Black Man of the Nile and his Family*, Alkebulan Books, N.Y., 1981.
Bernal, M., *Black Athena*, Vol. I: *The Fabrication of Ancient Greece 1785–1985*, Free Association Books, London, 1987.
Bohm, D., *The Special Theory of Relativity*, W.A. Benjamin Inc., N.Y., 1965.
Booth, N.S., *African Religions*, Nok Publishers, N.Y., Lagos, 1977.
Breasted, J., *Dawn of Conscience*, 1934.
Budge, E.A.W., *The Egyptian Book of the Dead*, Dover, N.Y., 1967.
Budge, E.A.W., *The Egyptian Religion*, RKP, 1979.
Budge, E.A.W., *The Gods of the Egyptians*, Dover, 1964.
Cabral, A., *Return to the Source: Selected Speeches*, Monthly Review Press, London & N.Y., 1973.
Carruthers, J.H., *Essays in Ancient Egyptian Studies*, Timbuctu Publishers, L.A., 1984.
Churchward, A., *Signs and Symbols of Primordial Man*, Greenwood Press, Westport, Conn.,1978.
Collard, A. and J. Contrucci, *Rape of the Wild*, Women's Press, London, 1987.
Cornford, F.M., *The Republic of Plato*, Oxford University Press, Oxford, 1941.
Davidson, B., *The Africans*, Longman, Harlow, 1969.
Diop, C.A., *African Origin of Civilization: Myth or Reality?*, Lawrence Hill & Co., Conn., 1974.
Diop, C.A., *The Cultural Unity of Black Africa*, Karnak House, London, 1989.
Easwaran, E., *The Dhammapada*, Arkana, London, 1987.
Einstein, A.. and L. Infield, *The Evolution of Physics*, Cambridge University Press, Cambridge, 1971.
Fanon, F., *Black Skin, White Masks*, Grove Press, N.Y., 1967.
Flew, A., *A Dictionary of Philosophy*, Pan Books, 1979.
Forde, D., ed., *African Worlds*, Oxford University Press, Oxford, 1954.
Frazer, J.G., *The Golden Bough*, Macmillan, London, 1983.

Frege, G., *The Foundations of Arithmetic*, Basil Blackwell, Oxford, 1980.
Gablik, S., *Has Modernism Failed?*, Thames & Hudson, London, 1984.
Griaule, M., *Conversations with Ogotemmeli*, Oxford University Press, Oxford, 1955.
Grunbaum, A., *The Philosophical Problems of Space and Time*, RKP, London, 1964.
Hountondji, P.J., *African Philosophy: Myth or Reality*, Hutchinson University Library for Africa, London, 1983.
Imasogie, O., *African Traditional Religions*, Ibadan University, Ibadan, 1985.
Jahn, J., *Muntu*, Faber and Faber, London, 1961.
James, G.G.M., *Stolen Legacy*, The African Publication Society, N.Y., 1971.
Jinadu, L.A., *Fanon: In Search of the African Revolution*, Fourth Dimension Publishers, Nigeria, 1980.
Kac, M. and S. Ulam, *Mathematics and Logic*, Penguin, Middlesex, 1979.
Kant, I., *Critique of Pure Reason*, Everyman, 1934.
Karenga, M., *The Husia*, Kawaida Publications, L.A., 1984.
Karenga, M., and J. Carruthers, eds., *Kemet and the African Worldview*, University of Sankore Press, L.A., 1986.
Karenga, M, "Towards a Sociology of Maatian Ethics," in Van Sertina, I., ed., *Egypt Revisited*, Journal of African Civilizations, New Jersey, 1989.
Kaufman, W.J., *Cosmic Frontiers of Relativity*, Penguin, 1979.
Leakey, L.S.B., '*The Evolution of Man on the African Continent*', Tarikh Vol. I, No. 3: *Man in Africa*, Longman, 1966.
Martin, Tony, *Race First: The Ideological and Organizational Struggles of Marcus Garvey and the Universal Negro Improvement Association*, Majority Press, Mass., 1976.
Mbiti, J.S., *African Religions and Philosophy*, Heinemann, London, 1969.
- -, *Introduction to African Religion*, Heinemann, London, 1975.
Metuh, E..I., *God and Man in African Religion*, Geoffrey Chapman, London, 1981.
Nauman, St. Elmo, *Dictionary of Asian Philosophies*, RKP, London, 1979.
Nketia, J.H., *The Music of Africa*, Victor Gollancz, London, 1975.
Nkrumah, K., *Consciencism*, Panaf Books, London, 1964.
Parrinder, E.G., *African Traditional Religion*, Oxford University Press, Oxford, 1974.
Parrinder, E.G., *The World's Living Religions*, Pan, London, 1964.

Piaget, J., *The Origin of Intelligence in the Child*, RKP, London, 1953.
Popper, K., *Conjectures and Refutations*, RKP, London, 1963.
Reed, B., *Rebel in the Soul: A Sacred Text of Ancient Egypt*, Wildwood House, London, 1978.
Rucker, R., *Infinity and the Mind*, Paladin Books, London, 1984.
Russel, B., *History of Western Philosophy*, Allen and Unwin, London, 1961.

Russel, B., *Why I am not a Christian*, Unwin Paperbacks, London, 1979.
Sartre, J.P., *Being and Nothingness*, Methuen and Co., London, 1943.
Schwaller de Lubicz, R.A., *Symbol and the Symbolic*, Inner Traditions International, N.Y., 1949.
Segy, L., *African Sculpture*, Dover, N.Y., 1958.
Segy, L., *Masks of Black Africa*, Dover, N.Y., 1976.
Tempels, P., *Bantu Philosophy*, Presence Africaine, Paris, 1959.
Thompson, G., *The Human Essence – The Sources of Science and Art*, China Policy Studies Group, London, 1974.
Tompkins, P., *Secrets of the Great Pyramids*, Allen Lane, 1973.
Van Sertima, I., ed., *Blacks in Science – Ancient and Modern*, Journal of African Civilizations, Transaction Books, 1985.
Vernon, M.D., *The Psychology of Perception*, Penguin, 1962.
Williams, C., *Destruction of Black Civilizations*, Third World Press, Illinois, 1976.
Wingert, P.S., *Primitive Art*, Meridian, N.Y., 1962.
Yates, F.A., *Giordano Bruno and the Hermetic Tradition*, RKP, London, 1964.
Zaslavsky, C., *Africa Counts: Number and Pattern in African Culture*, Lawrence Hill & Co., Conn., 1979.